Windows® 95
Clear & Simple™

Clear & Simple™ *Computer Books*

● easy to follow   ● jargon free   ● practical   ● task based   ● easy steps

Thousands of people have already discovered that the CLEAR & SIMPLE series gives them what they want *fast!* These are the books for you if you want to learn quickly what's essential and how to do things with a particular piece of software.

If you:

- Need to learn Windows 95
- Want to get the job done quickly and efficiently
- Need a self-teaching approach
- Want results fast

For clarity and simplicity, the CLEAR & SIMPLE Computer Books stand above all others.

This best selling series is in your local bookstore now, or in case of difficulty, contact: Manager of Special Sales, Butterworth-Heinemann, 313 Washington Street, Newton, MA 02158-1626   Tel: (617) 928-2500.

Series titles:

Windows 95	P.K. McBride	0 7506 9800 4
The Internet for Windows 95	P.K.McBride	0 7506 9801 2
Excel for Windows 95	Stephen Morris	0 7506 9802 0
Word for Windows 95	Keith Brindley	0 7506 9803 9

Windows® 95
Clear & Simple™

The HSUS

P.K.McBride

Ms Isabel Schoenemann
5 Post Ave Apt 21
New York, NY 10034-5841

nov. 4, 1997

Butterworth-Heinemann

Boston● Oxford● Johannesburg● Melbourne● New Delhi● Singapore

Library of Congress Cataloging-in-Publication Data
McBride, P.K.
      Windows 95 clear & simple / P.K. McBride
         p.   cm.
      Includes index.
      ISBN 0-7506-9800-4 (pbk.)
      1. Microsoft Windows (Computer file) 2. Operating systems (Computers) T. Title.
QA76,78.063M3743   1996
005.4'469--oo20   96-3198
                                          CIP

British Library Cataloguing-in-Publication Data
A catalogue record of this book is available from the British Library.

The publisher offers discounts on bulk orders of this book. For information, please write:
Manager of Special Sales
Butterworth—Heinemann
313 Washington Street
Newton, MA 02158-1626
Tel: 617-928-2500
Fax: 617-928-2620

For information on all Clear & Simple publications available, contact our World Wide Web home page at: http://www.bh.com/bh/

Order number: EY—XXXE—DP

10 9 8 7 6 5 4 3

Printed in the United States of America

Designed and Typeset by P.K. McBride, Southampton, UK
Archtype, Bash Casual, Cotswold and Gravity fonts from Advanced Graphics Ltd.
Icons designed by Sarah Ward © 1994

Contents

Preface

Many of you who are using or are about to start using Windows 95 will have previously used Windows 3.1. You will find many similarities in this new system, but you will also find that quite a number of the old concepts and ways of working no longer hold true. A few of you will have been working with MS-DOS or even OS/2. For some – and an increasing number as time goes on – it will be your first experience of a computer operating system.

I have tried to write with all of you in mind, and that has not been as difficult as it may sound. I believe that the best way to approach Windows 95 is to forget anything you may know about Windows 3.1 and start from scratch. If you insist on hanging on to your Windows 3.1 baggage, it will just slow you down – you will keep trying to do things the old way, and get frustrated because some won't work. However, your hard-won Windows 3.1 experience will not be wasted, for when you do find things that are similar to what you were used to, you will pick them up very quickly.

Here's a reassuring thought for anyone still doubtful about switching. This book was written and typeset on a system running Windows 95. It has proved to be more reliable, easier to use and quicker than was Windows 3.1.

1 Setting up

Before you start..

...ask yourself, "Do I really want to do this?" If your system is working perfectly well under Windows 3.1, why should you change to Windows 95?

There are some very good reasons:

- Windows 3.1 is a fancy front-end that uses DOS to do the dirty work – Windows 95 is an integrated system. By cutting out DOS, programs run faster!

- Windows 3.1 used 16-bit for much of its data transfer –Windows 95 is fully 32-bit. Data moves faster!

- Windows 95 has broken through the old DOS 640k limit, so that all parts of the available memory can be accessed just as easily. Task switching is faster!

- The new Desktop gives quicker access to your most commonly used programs and easier switching between windows. You work faster!

- Windows 95 is truly multi-tasking, capable of printing or running a database query (or both) while you are working in another application. Jobs get done faster!

- Built-in network and communications support gives simple access to the Internet and to sending and receiving faxes and e-mail – with a suitable modem.

- The new Plug and Play approach to hardware will make it easier to add new components to your system.

- Long filenames – breaching the old 8-character plus extension limit – identify files more clearly.

And why not?

- ❏ Some Windows 3.1 and DOS programs will not work with Windows 95 – one of your favorites might be among these.

- ❏ Despite the massive testing program, there may still be some bugs in the first edition.

- ❏ You may need a more powerful PC to run Windows 95.

The platform

Theoretical minimum

    386 processor
    4 Mb RAM
    100Mb hard drive
    Floppy disk

Practical minimum

    486 processor
    8 Mb RAM
    300 Mb hard disk
    CD-ROM
    Sound card

Basic steps

1 Either backup or copy the old DOS and Windows directories to a safe place.

2 Create a System disk.

3 Make WINDOWS and DOS directories on the floppy and copy in any essential files.

4 Copy onto it the AUTOEXEC.BAT and CONFIG.SYS files. Edit these so they run the programs on the floppy; e.g.

A:\DOS\SHARE.EXE /l:500

A:\WINDOWS\SMARTDRV.EXE

❑ Recovery

1 Restart from your system disk.

2 Delete the WINDOWS and DOS directories.

3 Copy the old ones back.

4 Sell this book.

Preparing for the worst

If your system may not be able to cope with Windows 95, or you use specialist software that may not be compatible, you must be able to reinstall Windows 3.1. Windows 95 prepares for this by making a compressed copy of the files from your DOS and WINDOWS directories, and providing an UNINSTALL utility. You should be able to run SETUP again and use this to remove Windows 95 and restore your old files. However, if you want to be on the safe side, it wouldn't hurt to make your own preparations.

To do this, you need a system disk with a full set of start-up files. Include copies of all the programs that are run from AUTOEXEC.BAT and CONFIG.SYS, so that you can do a proper start-up from the system disk. You should also copy (not move) your DOS, WINDOWS and WINDOWS/SYSTEM directories onto a second drive, if present, or into a new directory (perhaps called OLDSETUP). This would also be a good time to do a full backup onto a tape streamer, removable hard disk or set of floppies.

If Windows 95 doesn't do what you want, you can get back to Windows 3.1 without too much trouble.

The Setup Wizard

Setting up Windows 95 is largely a matter of responding to prompts as the Setup Wizard runs its course. However, there are a few points to watch out for.

- Allow at least an hour for installation – the Wizard may be able to do its stuff in 30 minutes, but you have to make some decisions, and that takes time.

- Accept all suggested settings, except for the few pointed out in the Steps.

- There are three main Setup options – Typical is the right one for most people; Compact will save a few Mb of space; Portable adds utilities for transferring data to and from portable PCs.

- Installing all the Components takes around 75Mb of space; cutting out the Accessories, Networking and other optional extras reduces this to under 40Mb.

- Don't install the Mail unless you are on a network.

- Do accept the offer of making a Startup disk. You may need it some day.

Double that!

1 Close down all applications except File Manager.

2 Find and run the SETUP.EXE program on your installation disks or CD-ROM.

3 Accept the defaults and keep clicking `Next >` until you reach Setup Options. Do you want a *Typical*, *Compact* or *Portable* setup?

4 At the Windows Components panel it is simplest to go for the most common option. You can add and remove components later when Windows is running.

5 If you want to make your own selection now, see page 6.

6 When the Wizard reaches the file copying stage, go for a coffee. It won't need you for a while.

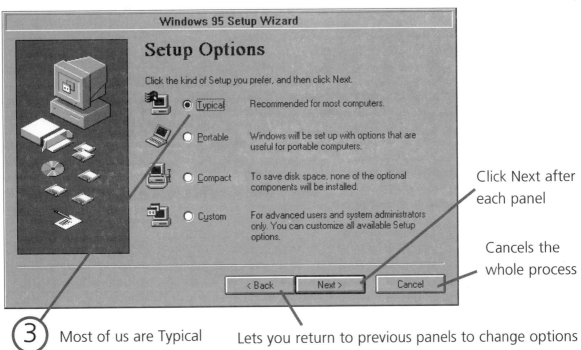

Windows 95 Setup Wizard

Setup Options

Click the kind of Setup you prefer, and then click Next.

- ⦿ Typical — Recommended for most computers.
- ◯ Portable — Windows will be set up with options that are useful for portable computers.
- ◯ Compact — To save disk space, none of the optional components will be installed.
- ◯ Custom — For advanced users and system administrators only. You can customize all available Setup options.

[< Back] [Next >] [Cancel]

Click Next after each panel

Cancels the whole process

③ Most of us are Typical

Lets you return to previous panels to change options

Tip

If the system appears to hang at times, don't panic. Each step takes longer than you think.

Windows 95 Setup Wizard

Windows Components

Windows comes with a variety of optional components, including games, mail, The Microsoft Network, and other accessories. Setup can install these now, or you can install them later from Control Panel.

Some options require extra disk space and won't be installed unless you choose them from the list.

Click the option you want, and then click Next.

- ⦿ Install the most common components (recommended)
- ◯ Show me the list of components so I can choose

[< Back] [Next >] [Cancel]

④ Let the Wizard make the basic selection

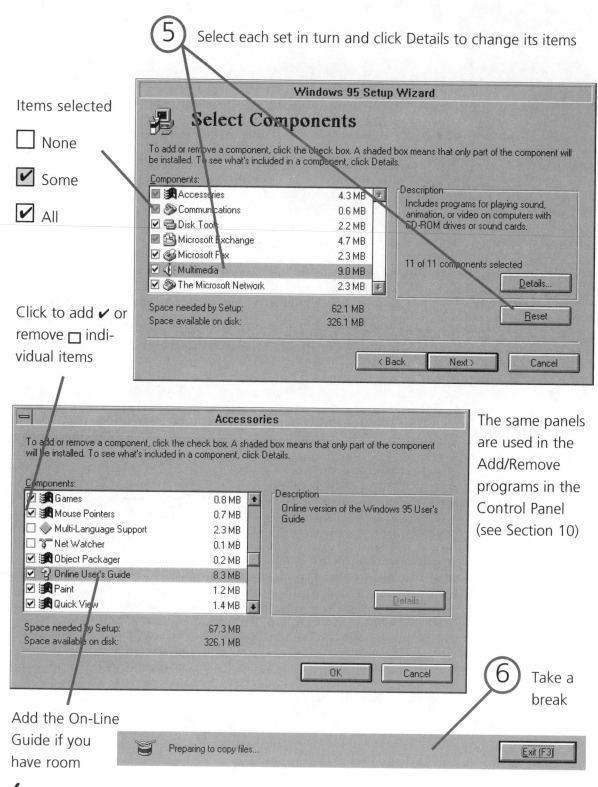

⑤ Select each set in turn and click Details to change its items

Items selected

☐ None

☑ Some

☑ All

Click to add ✔ or remove ☐ individual items

Windows 95 Setup Wizard

Select Components

To add or remove a component, click the check box. A shaded box means that only part of the component will be installed. To see what's included in a component, click Details.

Components:

☑ Accessories	4.3 MB	
☑ Communications	0.6 MB	
☑ Disk Tools	2.2 MB	
☑ Microsoft Exchange	4.7 MB	
☑ Microsoft Fax	2.3 MB	
☑ Multimedia	9.0 MB	
☑ The Microsoft Network	2.3 MB	

Description
Includes programs for playing sound, animation, or video on computers with CD-ROM drives or sound cards.

11 of 11 components selected

Details...

Space needed by Setup: 62.1 MB
Space available on disk: 326.1 MB

Reset

< Back   Next >   Cancel

Accessories

To add or remove a component, click the check box. A shaded box means that only part of the component will be installed. To see what's included in a component, click Details.

Components:

☑ Games	0.8 MB	
☑ Mouse Pointers	0.7 MB	
☐ Multi-Language Support	2.3 MB	
☐ Net Watcher	0.1 MB	
☑ Object Packager	0.2 MB	
☑ Online User's Guide	8.3 MB	
☑ Paint	1.2 MB	
☑ Quick View	1.4 MB	

Description
Online version of the Windows 95 User's Guide

Details...

Space needed by Setup: 67.3 MB
Space available on disk: 326.1 MB

OK   Cancel

The same panels are used in the Add/Remove programs in the Control Panel (see Section 10)

⑥ Take a break

Add the On-Line Guide if you have room

Preparing to copy files...

Exit (F3)

Taking the Tour

Tip

Check out What's New on the Welcome screen for a quick overview of the new features of Windows 95.

When the PC restarts, running Windows 95 for the first time, it will take a while to get going. Be patient – it's got a lot to think about. You will know you are there when you see the Welcome screen. If you have Windows 95 on CD, you will be offered the Tour. Take it! It only lasts a few minutes, but it will make you aware of some of the possibilities and features of the system.

Click this during the Tour to get back to the main menu

Exit at any point

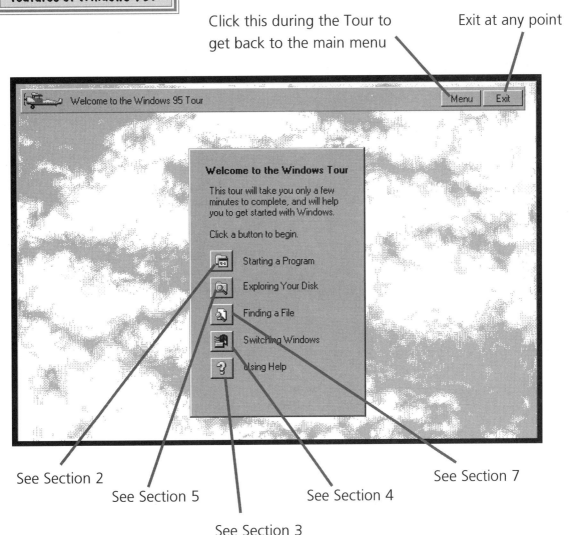

See Section 2

See Section 5

See Section 3

See Section 4

See Section 7

Summary

❑ Windows 95 is a more advanced system than Windows 3.1 but needs a more powerful PC.

❑ Most, but not all, existing Windows and DOS software will run under Windows 95.

❑ If worse comes to worst, you can uninstall WIndows 95 and restore your old system.

❑ Installation is a slow process, but easy to do, thanks to the Wizard.

❑ You can use one of the predefined Setups or make your own selection of components.

❑ The Tour takes only a few moments, but gives a useful overview of Windows 95.

2 Start here

The Desktop

Windows 95 is a Graphical User Interface (or GUI, pronounced *gooey*). What this means is that you work mainly by pointing at and clicking on symbols on the screen, rather than by typing commands. It is largely intuitive – i.e. the obvious thing to do is probably the right thing, and it is tolerant of mistakes. Many can be corrected as long as you tackle them straight away, and many others can be corrected easily, even after time has passed.

One of the ideas behind the design of Windows and of most Windows applications is that you should treat the screen as you would a desk. This is where you lay out your papers and books and tools, to suit your own way of working. You may want to have more than one set of papers on the desktop at a time – so Windows lets you run several programs at once. You may want to have all your papers visible, for comparing or transferring data; you may want to concentrate on one, but have the others at hand. These – and other arrangements – are all possible.

Each program runs in its own window, and these can be arranged side by side, overlapping, or with the one you are working on filling the desktop and the others tucked out of the way, but still instantly accessible.

Just as there are many ways of arranging your desktop, so there are many ways of working with it – in fact, you are sometimes spoiled for choice!

It's your desktop. How you arrange it, and how you use it is up to you. This book will show you the simplest ways to use Windows 95 effectively.

❑ What you see on screen when you start Windows depends upon the Desktop settings and shortcuts that you are using.

❑ What the screen looks like once you are into your working session, is infinitely variable.

❑ Certain principles always apply and certain things are always there. It is the fact that all Windows applications share a common approach that makes Windows so easy to use.

Desktop – you can change the background
pattern and the colors that are used.

Shortcuts – instant access to
programs. You can create your
own shortcuts.

Program windows – adjust their
size and placing to suit yourself.

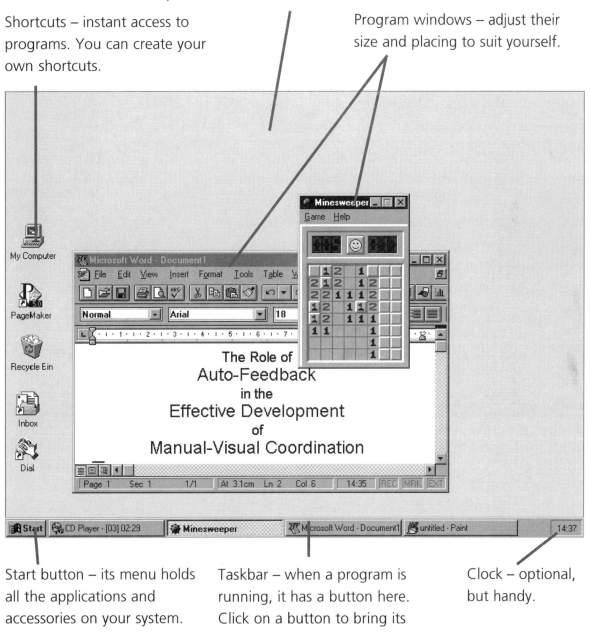

Start button – its menu holds
all the applications and
accessories on your system.

Taskbar – when a program is
running, it has a button here.
Click on a button to bring its
program to the top.

Clock – optional,
but handy.

Taming the mouse

You can't do much in Windows until you have tamed the mouse. It is used for locating the cursor, for selecting from menus, highlighting, moving and changing the size of objects, and much more. It won't bite, but it will wriggle until you have shown it who's in charge.

To control the mouse effectively you need a mouse mat or a thin pad of paper – mice don't run well on hard desktops.

The mouse and the cursor

Moving the mouse rolls the ball inside it. The ball turns the sensor rollers and these transmit the movement to the cursor. Straightforward? Yes, but note these points.

- If you are so close to the edge of the mat that you cannot move the cursor any further, pick up the mouse and plonk it back into the middle. If the ball doesn't move, the cursor doesn't move.

- You can set up the mouse so that when the mouse is moved faster, the cursor moves further. (See *Adjusting the mouse*, page 116.) Watch out for this when working on other people's machines.

Tip

A clean mouse is a happy mouse. If it starts to act up, take out the ball and clean it and the rollers with a damp tissue. Check for fluff build-up on the roller axles and remove any with tweezers.

Mouse actions

Point Move the cursor with your fingers off the buttons.

Click the left button to select a file, menu item or other object.

Click the right button to open a short menu of commands that apply to that object.

Double click to run programs. You can set the gap between clicks to suit yourself. (See *Adjusting the mouse*, page 116.)

Drag Keep the left button down while moving the mouse. Used for resizing, drawing and similar jobs.

Drag and drop Drag an object and release the button when it is in the right place. Used for moving objects.

Key guide

[Esc] – to Escape from trouble. Use it to cancel bad choices.

[Tab] – often used to move between objects on screen.

[Caps Lock] – only put this on when you want to type a lot of capitals. The Caps Lock light shows if it is on.

[Shift] – use it for capitals and the symbols on the number keys.

[Ctrl] – often used with other keys to give keystroke alternatives to mouse commands.

[Alt] – used, like [Ctrl], in combination with other keys.

[Backspace] – erases the character to the left of the text cursor.

[Enter] – used at the end of a piece of text or to start an operation.

[Delete] – deletes files, folders and screen objects. Use with care.

The keyboard

Most Windows 95 operations can be handled quite happily by the mouse alone, leaving the keyboard for data entry. However, keys are necessary for some jobs, and if you prefer typing to mousing, it is possible to do most jobs from the keyboard. The relevant ones are shown here.

The function keys

Many operations can be run from these – if you can be bothered to learn the keystrokes. The only one really worth remembering is [F1]. This will always call up Help.

The control sets

The Arrow keys can often be used instead of the mouse for moving the cursor. Above them are more movement keys, which will let you jump around in text. [Insert] and [Delete] are also here. (See the Key guide.)

Escape   Caps Lock   Movement

 Tab   Delete

         F1- Help   Enter   Num Lock

                  Alt   Shift   Arrows   Enter

       Shift   Ctrl   Number Pad

Ctrl   *Numbers with NumLock ON*

Making choices

There are many situations where you have to specify a filename or an option. Sometimes you have to type in what you want, but in most cases, it only takes a click of the mouse or a couple of keystrokes.

Menus

To pull one down from the menu bar click on it, or press [Alt] and the underlined letter – usually the initial.

To select an item from a menu, click on it or type its underlined letter.

Some items are *toggles*. Selecting them turns an option on or off. ✔ beside the name shows that the option is on.

▶ after an item shows that another menu leads from it.

If you select an item with three dots ... after it, a dialog box will open to get more information from you.

Dialog boxes

These vary, but will usually have:

●   OK   to click when you have set the options, selected the file or whatever;

●   Apply   fix the options selected so far, but not leave the box;

●   Cancel   in case you decide the whole thing was a mistake;

●   Help   or 🔳 to get help on items in the box.

Click or press [Alt]-[V]

Sub-menu

Toggle

Dialog box will follow

Click to get to its panel

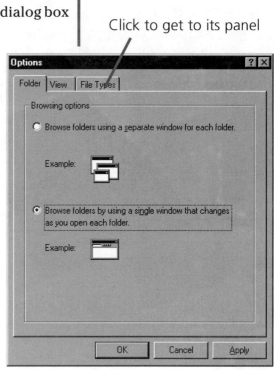

Tabs and panels

Some dialog boxes have several sets of options in them, each on a separate panel. These are identified by tabs at the top. Click on a tab to bring its panel to the front. Usually clicking OK on any panel will close the whole box. Use Apply when you have finished with one panel but want to explore others before closing.

Check boxes

These are used where there are several options, and you can use as many as you like at the same time.

✔ in the box shows that the option has been selected.

If the box is gray and the caption faint, the option is not available for the selected item.

Only this one

Not available

Radio buttons

These are used for either/or options. Only one of the set can be selected.

The selected option is shown by black blob in the middle.

This one please

Drop-down lists

If a slot has a down arrow button on its right, click the button to drop down a list.

Click on an item in the list to select.

Click here...

... to get the list

Welcome!

When Windows 95 starts up, it first displays a friendly welcome. The Did you know... tip is different every time and can be very useful, but after a few sessions you may feel that you have been welcomed enough. When you reach that point, you can stop it from reappearing.

Take the tour (page 7) – needs the installation CD-ROM

See the main changes from Windows 3.1

Read the ads – this needs the installation CD-ROM

Display another tip

Go to work

Click to close

Click to remove ✔ and turn off the Welcome displays

What's New? Click to read the topic – see Section 3 for more on Help

The Start menu

Clicking on **Start** at the bottom left of the screen, takes you into the menu system from which you can run applications, get help, find files, customize your system and close down at the end of a session.

The first level menu has 7 options:

Programs is the main route to your applications. It is the equivalent of Program Manager in Windows 3.1. Leading from this is a second level of program folders, and selecting from there takes you to the icons for the programs in each folder.

Documents holds a list of recently used document files. Selecting one from this list will run the relevant application and open the file for you to work on.

Settings is used to customize the desktop and other aspects of the system (Section 10), set up printers (Section 11) and even rewrite the menu (Section 9).

Find will track down files and folders on your computer – and on your local network or the Microsoft Network if you are connected.

Help is one way into the Help system (Section 3).

Run lets you run a named application or starts up work on a document. You would mainly use this for installing new software or for handling a file that you have brought in on a floppy disk.

Shut down is the only safe way to end a session.

Running a program

If you know where a program is in the menu structure, running it should take no more than a few mouse moves and clicks. Even if you do not know where it is, it will take only a few moments longer to browse through the menus to find and run it.

Basic steps

1   Click ▓Start

2   Point to Programs. The program folder menu opens.

3   Point to the folder that contains the program – if you cannot see it in that menu, point to another item and check its menu.

❑   You may have to repeat Step 3 as some folders have other folders within them.

4   Click once on the program to run it.

Next level menu

Click to run

③ Point to the folder

② Point to Programs

① Click Start

Take note

Any applications that were on your PC before you installed Windows 95 should have been brought into the Start menu; any that came in with Windows 95 will be there; any that you install later should slot themselves into the menus, and you can add others at any time.

Basic steps

1 Click ▓Start▓

2 Point to Documents.

3 Click on the file to get started on it.

Icons and extensions

 AVI – multimedia

 BMP – Bitmap graphic

 DOC – Word for Windows

 TTF – True Type Font

 TXT – Plain text file

 XLS – Excel spreadsheet

 ZIP – WinZip compressed file

Working from documents

The Documents item on the Start menu brings up a list of files that you have recently used. Selecting one of these will start the relevant application and load in the document.

There is room for 15 documents in the list. Once you hit the limit, new documents push out the oldest ones.

Each document is accompanied by a little icon, to help identify the type of file. There must be hundreds of different icons, but you will soon come to recognize those of types that you use regularly. A few of the more common ones are listed on the right.

Take note

You can run programs directly or through document files from Explorer. See pages 78 and 80.

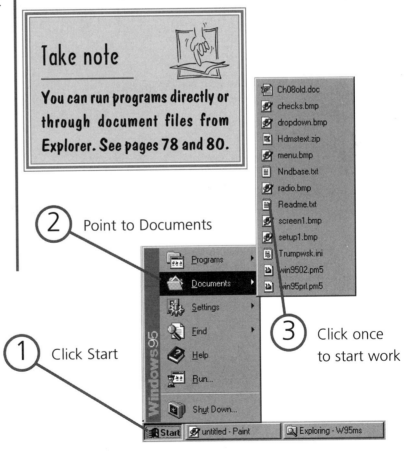

② Point to Documents

① Click Start

③ Click once to start work

19

Short menus

If you click the right button on almost anything on screen in Windows 95, a short menu will open beside it. This contains a set of commands and options that can be applied to the object.

What is on the menu depends upon the type of object. Three are shown here to give an idea of the possibilities.

Properties

Most menus have a Properties item. The contents of its dialog box also vary according to the nature of the object. For shortcuts, like the one for the Phone Dialer shown below, there is a *Shortcut* panel that controls the link to the program. The (hidden)*General*panel has a description of the file – this panel is in every file's Properties box.

Files can be Opened, Sent to a removable disk or off in the mail, and Deleted – among other things.

The Clock can be adjusted, and as it is on the Taskbar, you can also arrange the screen display from this menu.

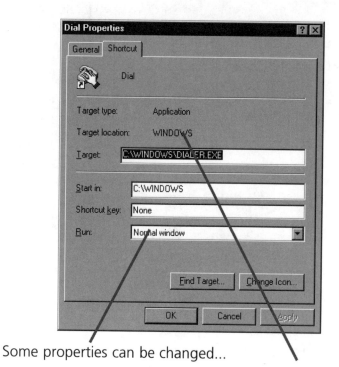

Some properties can be changed...

...others are there for information only

Help pages can be Printed or Annotated – you can even adjust the Font size.

Basic steps

Shutting down

1 Click **Start**

2 Click Shut down.

3 If you want to restart, set the option.

4 Click Yes.

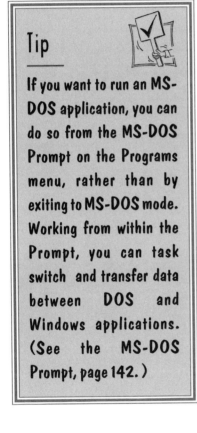

Tip

If you want to run an MS-DOS application, you can do so from the MS-DOS Prompt on the Programs menu, rather than by exiting to MS-DOS mode. Working from within the Prompt, you can task switch and transfer data between DOS and Windows applications. (See the MS-DOS Prompt, page 142.)

When you have finished work on your computer, you must shut it down properly, and not just turn it off. This is essential. During your work session, applications and Windows 95 may have created temporary work files – including the swap file which can get very large if you run several applications at once. Data files that you have been editing may still be open in a memory buffer and not yet written safely to disk. An organized shut down closes and stores open files and clears away unwanted ones.

Sometimes you will find that a bug in an application or in Windows 95 has made the system hang or otherwise misbehave. Press [Ctrl]-[Alt]-[Delete] together to close that application, then shut down and restart. That generally clears most problems.

③ Restart?

④ Click Yes

If you start a shut down by mistake – easily done – you can stop it

① Click Start

② Choose Shut down

Summary

❑ Windows is an intuitive system – if something *feels* right, it probably *is* right.

❑ All Windows software works in much the same way, so once you have got the hang of one program, you are half way to learning the next.

❑ The mouse is an important tool. Practice using it – a good excuse for playing the games!

❑ Some operations are easier with keys, and just a few can only be done from the keyboard.

❑ Selections can usually be made by picking from a list or clicking on a button or check box.

❑ The Start button is the main way into the system. Get to know your way around its menus.

❑ Applications can be run directly from the Programs menu, or through files in the Documents list.

❑ Every object has a short menu of common commands that can be used with it.

❑ You must shut down properly at the end of a session.

3 Help!

Help topics

You can get help in several different ways:

- The main Help topics, run from the Start menu;

- Help topics on applications and accessories, run from their menus;

- Query help on dialog boxes;

In all Help topics systems there are three approaches:

- an organized Contents list;

- Indexed Help pages;

- a word-based Find facility.

Basic steps

❑ From the Desktop

1 Click

2 Click on Help.

❑ From an application

1 Click on Help on the menu bar.

2 Select Help Topics.

① Open the Help menu

② Select Help Topics

② Select Help

① Open the Start menu

Take note

Windows 3.1 applications have a slightly different Help menu. In these, select Help – Contents to get to the topics pages. The Index and Find facilities are reached through Help – Search.

Tip

You can press [F1] – anywhere, any time – to get into the Help system.

Basic steps

Contents

1 Click the Contents tab if this panel is not at the front already.

2 Point to ◆ and click [Display] to see the page titles.

3 Point to [?] and click [Display] to read the page.

either

4 Click Help Topics to return to the Contents panel.

or

5 Click [×] to close the page and exit Help.

This approach treats the Help pages as a book. You scan through the headings to find a section that seems to cover what you want, and open that to see the page titles. (Some sections have sub-sections, making it a 2 or 3 stage process to get to page titles.)

Some Help topics are stand-alone pages; others have Related topics buttons to take you on to further pages.

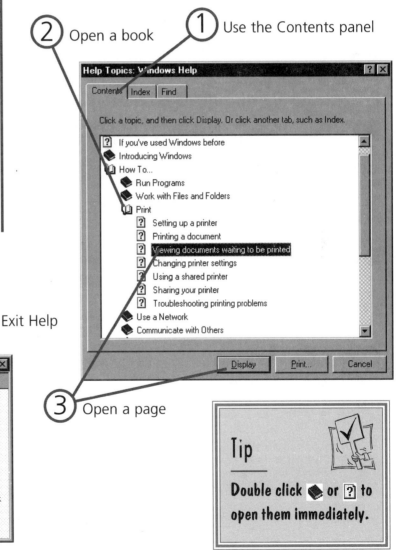

② Open a book   ① Use the Contents panel

③ Open a page

④ Go back for more

⑤ Exit Help

Tip

Double click ◆ or [?] to open them immediately.

25

Using the Index

Though the Contents are good for getting an overview of how things work, if you want help on a specific problem – usually the case – you are better off with the Index.

This is organized through a cross-referenced list of terms. The main list is alphabetical, with sub-entries, just like the index in a book. And, as with an index in a book, you can plow through it slowly from the top, or skip through to find the words that start with the right letters. Once you find a suitable entry, you can display the list of cross-referenced topics and pick one of those.

Basic steps

1 Click the Index tab.

2 Start to type a word into the slot to focus the entry list or use the scroll bar to find the topic.

3 Select the entry.

4 Click [Display]

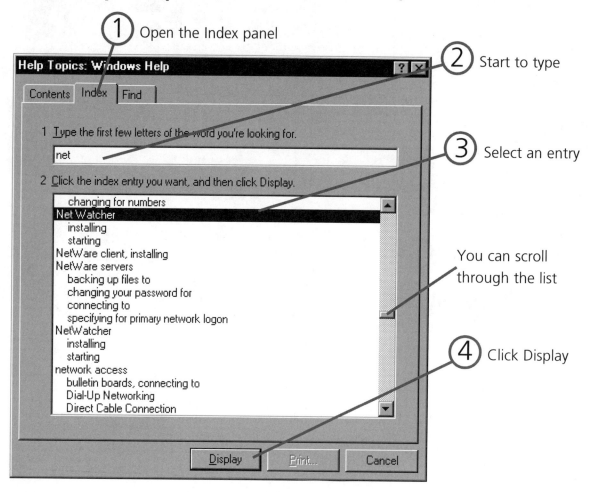

① Open the Index panel

② Start to type

③ Select an entry

You can scroll through the list

④ Click Display

26

5 Pick the most suitable topic from the Topics Found list.

6 Click [Display]

❏ The help page will open. When you have finished with it you can click Help Topics to return to the Index or ⊠ to close the page and exit Help.

Take note

When using Windows 3.1 applications, the Index panel is reached through Help – Search.

If you cannot see anything useful, close the panel and return to the Index

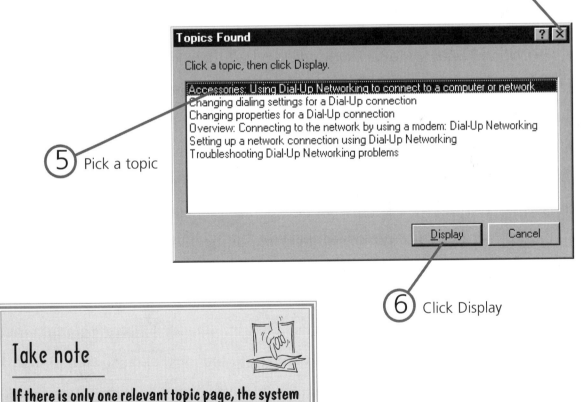

Topics Found   ? ⊠

Click a topic, then click Display.

Accessories: Using Dial-Up Networking to connect to a computer or network.
Changing dialing settings for a Dial-Up connection
Changing properties for a Dial-Up connection
Overview: Connecting to the network by using a modem: Dial-Up Networking
Setting up a network connection using Dial-Up Networking
Troubleshooting Dial-Up Networking problems

[Display]   [Cancel]

⑤ Pick a topic

⑥ Click Display

Take note

If there is only one relevant topic page, the system will bypass the Topics Found panel, and take you directly to the page after Step 4.

Finding help

If you can't track down the help you need from the Index, you can Find it using the third Help panel. This works by creating a list of all the words in the Help pages; you give it one or more words to search for and it produces a list of all the topics that contain matching words.

1 Open the Find panel in Help Topics.

2 Type your word into the top slot. As you type, words starting with the typed letters appear in the pane beneath.

3 If you want to narrow the search, go back to step 2, type a space after your first word and give another.

4 Select the most suitable word from the Narrow the search pane.

5 Select a topic from the lower pane.

6 Click [Display]

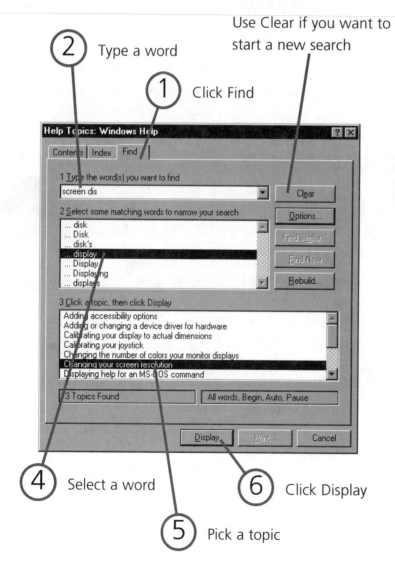

② Type a word

Use Clear if you want to start a new search

① Click Find

④ Select a word

⑥ Click Display

⑤ Pick a topic

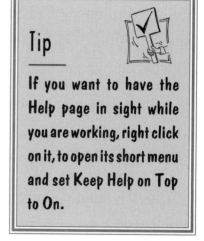

Tip

If you want to have the Help page in sight while you are working, right click on it, to open its short menu and set Keep Help on Top to On.

28

Basic steps

Find options

□ Narrowing the scope

1 On the Find panel, click
   [Options...]

2 On the Find Options
   panel, click [Files...]

□ This shows a list of the
   Help files that will be
   searched. Some of these
   are not relevant.

3 Hold [Ctrl] and click on
   the files that you want it
   to ignore. If you remove
   one by mistake, click
   again to reselect it.

4 Click [OK] then
   close the Options panel.

There are several Options that you can set to alter the
nature of the search or narrow its scope.

In the Search for words containing box, select

All the words... where you are using several words to
focus on one topic

At least one... where you are giving several alternatives in
the hope that it recognizes one

Are the words all part
of the definition or are
they alternatives?

Select this if you don't
want the word list to
change while you type

② Click Files

③ [Ctrl] and click to remove or reselect

④ Click OK

Take note

The first time you use Find
for Windows 95 or for any
application, a Wizard will
run to create the word list.
Take the Minimum option
— it's quicker, and detailed
enough for most of us.

Instant help

As well as the main Help system, Windows 95 offers a couple of other brief, but useful, forms of help.

The query icon

All dialog boxes and panels in Windows 95 and its components – and in newer applications – have an ? icon on the top right of the status bar. You will also find an ? icon on the toolbar of some applications. They can both be used for finding out more about objects on screen.

1 Click on the ? or 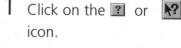 icon.

2 Click the ? cursor on the button, option or other item that you want to know about.

3 After you have read the help box, click anywhere to close it.

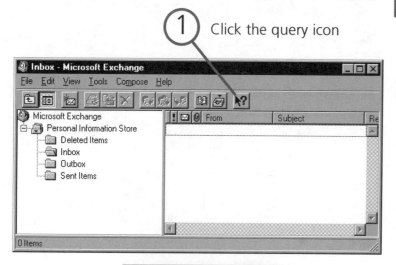

① Click the query icon

Take note

You only get one help box for each click on the query icon, though you can use that as often as you like.

① Click the query icon

② Get help where you want it

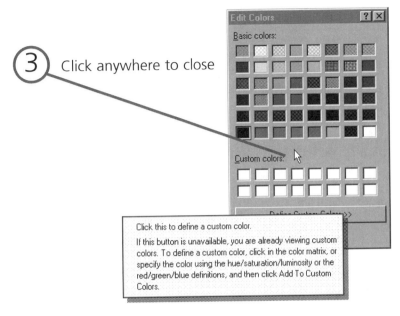

③ Click anywhere to close

Click this to define a custom color.

If this button is unavailable, you are already viewing custom colors. To define a custom color, click in the color matrix, or specify the color using the hue/saturation/luminosity or the red/green/blue definitions, and then click Add To Custom Colors.

Help on icons

Icons are supposed to be self-explanatory, but their purpose can not always be summed up in a small image. Never fear, help is near!

Point and wait to see the icon's label

Let the cursor rest over an icon for a moment and a label will pop up to tell you what it is. If that isn't enough to tell you what it does, at least you have a name to look up in the Help Index.

Summary

❑ Help is always available.

❑ Use the Contents panel when you are browsing to see what topics are covered.

❑ Use the Index to go directly to the help on a specified operation or object.

❑ If you can't locate the help in the Index, use the Find facility to track down the pages.

❑ In Windows 3.1 applications, Find is called Search.

❑ For help with items in a dialog box or panel, click the query icon and point to the item.

❑ If you hold the cursor over an icon, a brief prompt will pop up to tell you what it does.

4 Window control

The window frame

This is more than just a pretty border. It contains all the controls you need for adjusting the display.

Frame edge

This has a control system built into it. When a window is in Restore mode – i.e. smaller than full-screen – you can drag on the edge to make it larger or smaller. (See *Changing the size*, page 41.)

Title bar

This is to remind you of where you are and is used for moving the window. Drag on this and the window moves. (See *Moving windows*, page 40.)

Maximize, Minimize and Restore

These buttons change the display mode. Only one of Maximize and Restore will be visible at any one time. (See *Window modes*, page 36.)

Close

One of several ways to close a window and the program that was running in it. (See *Closing windows*, page 43.)

Control menu icon

There is no set image for this icon, as every application has its own, but clicking on whatever is in the far left of the title bar will open the Control menu. This can be used for changing the screen mode or closing the window. (See *Window modes*, page 36.) Double-clicking this icon will close down the window.

Take note

Most applications can handle several documents at once, each in its own window. These are used in almost the same way as program windows. The applications usually have a Window menu containing controls for the document windows.

Menu bar

Immediately below the Title bar in an application's window is a bar containing the names of its menus. Clicking on one of these will drop down a list of commands.

Scroll bars

These are present on the right side and bottom of the frame if the display contained by the window is too big to fit within it. The Sliders in the Scroll Bars show you where your view is, relative to the overall display. Moving these allows you to view a different part of the display. (See *Scrolling*, page 42.)

Window modes

All programs are displayed on screen in windows, and these can normally have three modes:

- Maximized – filling the whole screen;
- Minimized – not displayed, though still present as a button on the Task bar;
- Restore – adjustable in size and in position.

Maximized

In Restore mode

Minimized – not visible except for this

Basic steps

❏ To make a window full-screen

Click 🔲 or select Maximize from the Control Menu

❏ To restore a window to variable size

Click 🖼 or select Restore from the Control Menu

❏ To shrink a window to an icon

Click ⬛ or select Minimize from the Control Menu

Changing display modes

Clicking on the buttons in the top right corner of the frame is the simplest way to switch between Maximize and Restore modes, and to Minimize a window. If you prefer it can be done using the Control Menu.

The Control menu

Click the icon at the top left to open this. Options that they don't apply at the time will be "grayed out". The menu here came from a variable size window. One from a full-screen window would have Move, Size and Maximize in gray.

Using the Taskbar

Click a program's button to bring its window to the top.

Right click the button to open the Control menu.

Left click to activate

Right click for the menu

Keyboard Control

[Alt]–[Space] opens the Control menu of an application.

[Alt]–[-] (minus) opens the Control menu of a document.

Minimized documents

When you minimize a document window, within an application, it shrinks to a tiny title bar, with just enough room for an abbreviated name and the icons. Click Maximize or Restore to open it out again.

Restore   Maximize

Arranging windows

If you want to have two or more windows visible at the same time, you will have to arrange them on your desktop. There are Windows tools that will do it for you, or you can do it yourself.

If you right click the Taskbar, its menu has options to arrange the windows on the desktop. Open it and you will see Cascade, Tile Vertical and Tile Horizontal. Similar options are on the Window menu of most applications, though these only affect the layout *within* the programs.

- Cascade places the windows overlapping with just the title bars of the back ones showing. You might just as well Maximize the current window, and use the Taskbar buttons to get to the rest.

- Either of the Tile layouts can be the basis of a well-arranged desktop.

Basic steps

1 Maximize or Restore the windows that you want to include in the layout. Minimize those that you will not be using actively.

2 Right click the Taskbar to open its menu.

3 Select Tile Horizontal or Tile Vertical.

4 If you only want to work in one window at a time, Maximize it, and Restore it back into the arrangement when you have finished.

Tip

If you want to adjust the balance of the layout, you can move and resize the windows.

① Right click the Taskbar

② Select a Tile display

Cascade
Tile Horizontally
Tile Vertically
Minimize All Windows
Properties

Start | Aldus PageMaker 5.0 | untitled - Paint | 01:01

Tip

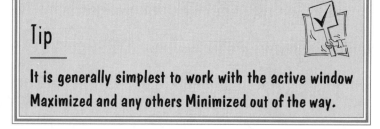

It is generally simplest to work with the active window Maximized and any others Minimized out of the way.

38

Tile

Tile displays are useful when copying between disks, as the limited view within each window does not make much difference

Tile arranges open windows side by side (Vertical), or in rows (Horizontal) – with more than three windows, the tiling is in both directions. As the window frames take up space, the actual working area is significantly reduced. You cannot do much serious typing in a tiled window.

The Taskbar menu now has an Undo Tile option to restore your screen to its previous state.

Moving windows

When a window is in Restore mode – open but not full screen – it can be moved anywhere on the screen.

● If you are not careful it can be moved almost off the screen! Fortunately, at least a bit of the title bar will still be visible, and that is the handle you need to grab to pull it back into view.

1 If the Title bar isn't highlighted, click on the window to make it the active one.

2 Point at the Title bar and hold the left button down.

3 Drag the window to its new position – you will only see a gray outline moving.

4 Release the button.

1 Make the Window active

2 Hold the pointer on the Title bar

3 Drag the outline

4 Release to drop into its new position

Basic steps

1 Move the pointer to the edge or corner that you want to pull in or out.

2 When you see the double-headed arrow, hold down the left mouse button and drag the outline to the required size.

3 Release the button.

When a window is in Restore mode, you can change its size and shape by dragging the edges of the frame to new positions.

Combined with the moving facility, this lets you arrange your desktop exactly the way you like it.

● The resize pointers only appear when the pointer is just on an edge, and they disapear again if you go too far. Practice! You'll soon get the knack of catching them.

You can drag any edge or corner

③ Drag the outline

④ Release

Tip

The quickest way to get a window the right size, in the right place, is to use the bottom right size handle to set the shape, then drag the window into position.

Scrolling

What you can see in a window is often only part of the story. The working area of the application may well be much larger. If there are scroll bars on the side and/or bottom of the window, this tells you that there is more material outside the frame. The scroll bars let you pull some of this material into view.

> ## Tip
>
> **If a window is blank – and you think there should be something there – push the sliders to the very top and left. That's where your work is likely to be.**

❑ Drag the Slider ▨ to scroll the view in the window. Keep your pointer moving straight along the bar or it won't work!

❑ Click an Arrow ▲ to edge the slider towards the arrow. Hold down for a slow continuous scroll.

❑ Click on the Bar beside the Slider to make it jump towards the pointer.

Sliders

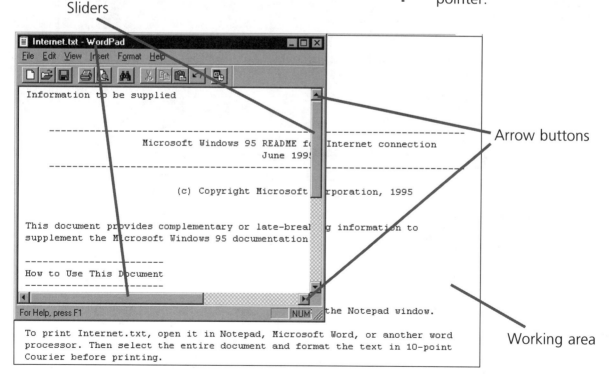

Arrow buttons

Working area

Basic steps

❏ Closing an active
window

1 Click ⊠

or

1 Press [Alt]-[F4].

❏ Closing from the
Taskbar

1 Right click the progam's
button to get its menu.

2 Select Close.

3 If you have forgotten to
save your work, take the
opportunity that is
offered to you.

When you close a window, you close down the program
that was running inside it.

If you haven't saved your work, most programs will point
this out and give you a chance to save before closing.

There are at least 5 different ways of closing. Here are the
simplest three:

● If the window is in Maximized or Restore mode, click
the close icon at the top right of the Title bar. (If
your mouse control is not too hot, you may well do
this when you are trying to Maximize the window!)

● If the window has been Minimized onto the Taskbar,
right click on its button to open the Control menu
and use Close.

● If you prefer working from keys, press [Alt]-[F4].

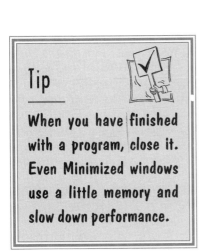

Tip

**When you have finished
with a program, close it.
Even Minimized windows
use a little memory and
slow down performance.**

① Click

② Close

① Right click

③ Save it?

Summary

❑ You can move between windows by clicking on any visible part of them – though the active parts of the frame should be avoided.

❑ Windows can be displayed in Maximized (full-screen) or Restore (variable-size) modes, or Minimized to icons.

❑ Minimized windows can be restored to full size by clicking on them.

❑ Windows can be arranged on the desktop by picking Cascade or Tile from the Task List options.

❑ A window can be moved about the screen by dragging on its title bar.

❑ You can change the size by dragging on any of its edges.

❑ The scroll bars will let you move the working area inside a window.

❑ Closing a window closes its program.

5 Exploring folders

Explorer v. My Computer

Explorer, My Computer and Network Neighborhood are you main file and folder management tools.

Explorer

This is closely related to File Manager of Windows 3.1. It gives a dual display, with the folder structure on the left and the contents of the current folder on the right.

Though Explorer will only display the contents of one folder – there is no multi-window display as in File Manager – you can run two or more copies of it at once. This can be useful when you are moving or copying files from one part of the system to another.

Explorer can access the folders in all of the drives attached to your computer, and to any that may be accessible to you over a network.

My Computer

This has a simpler display than Explorer. It works in a single-pane window, and when first opened it gives an overview of the components of your own system. You can then open another window to get a detailed look at folders in a drive, and continue opening further windows to go deeper into folders.

Though Explorer gives a clearer view than My Computer of how your storage is organized, My Computer probably gives you a clearer view of any one part of the system.

Network Neighborhood

This is the same as My Computer, but opens with the focus on any networked machines.

Take note

Whether you use Explorer or My Computer for your file management is up to you. I use either – and sometimes both at once – depending upon the job. As Explorer can do all that My Computer can do – and more – the examples in the following pages will all use Explorer. We will come back to My Computer at the end of the section.

The jargon

- ❏ Root – the folder of the disk. All other folders branch off from the root.

- ❏ Parent – a folder that contains another.

- ❏ Child – a sub-folder of a Parent.

- ❏ Branch – the structure of sub-folders open off from a folder.

Tip

When planning the folder structure, keep it simple. Too many folders within folders can make it hard to find files.

If you are going to work successfully with Windows 95 – or any computer system – you must understand how its disk storage is organized, and how to manage files efficiently and safely. In this section, we will look at the filing system, working with folders and the screen displays of Explorer and My Computer. In later sections, we will cover managing files and looking after your disks.

Folders

The hard disks supplied on modern PCs are typically 540 Megabytes or larger. A Megabyte is 1 million bytes and each byte can hold one character (or part of a number or graphic). That means that a typical hard disk can hold up to 80 million words – enough for 400 hefty novels! More to the point, if you were using it to store letters and reports, it could hold many thousands of files. It must be organized if you are ever to find your files.

Folders provide this organization. They are containers in which related files can be placed to keep them together, and away from other files. A folder can also contain sub-folders – which can themselves be subdivided. You can think of the first level of folders as being sets of filing cabinets; the second level are drawers within the cabinets, and the next level folders within the drawers. (And the folders could have subdividers – there is no limit to this.)

Paths

The structure of folders is often referred to as the tree. It starts at the root, which is the drive letter – C: for your main hard disk – and branches off from there.

A folder's position in the tree is described by its path. For most operations, you can identify a folder by clicking on it in a screen display, but now and then you will have to type its path. This should start at the drive letter and the root, and include every folder along the branch, with a backslash (\) between the names.

For example:

C:\DTP

C:\WORDPROC\LETTERS

When you want to know a path, look it up in the Explorer display and trace the branches down from the root.

Filenames

A filename has two parts – the name and an extension.

The name is no longer restricted to 8 characters, as it was in DOS and Windows 3.1. It can be as long as you like, and include any characters – including spaces. But don't let the freedom go to your head. The longer the name, the greater the opportunity for typing errors. The most important thing to remember when giving a filename is that it must mean something to you, so that you can find it easily next time you come back to the job.

The extension can be from 0 to 3 characters, and is separated from the rest of the name by a dot. It is used to identify the nature of the file. Windows and MS-DOS use the extensions COM, EXE, SYS, INI, DLL to identify special files of their own.

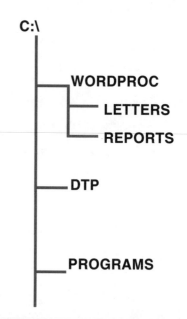

C:\
WORDPROC
LETTERS
REPORTS
DTP
PROGRAMS

Take note

Whatever you call a file, Windows 95 will also give it a name in the 8.3 MS-DOS format, for use with older applications.

The MS-DOS name will start with the same six letters, then have ~ and a number. "LETTER TO BILL.DOC' will become "LETTER~1.DOC"

Most applications also use their own special extensions. Word-processor files are often marked with DOC or TXT; spreadsheet files are usually WQ1 or WK1; database files typically have DB extensions.

If you are saving a file in a word-processor, spreadsheet or other application, and are asked for a filename, you normally only have to give the first part. The application will take care of the extension. If you do need to give an extension, make it meaningful. BAK is a good extension for backup files; TXT for text files.

When an application asks you for a filename – and the file is in the *current* folder – type in the name and extension only. If the file is in *another* folder, type in the path, a backslash separator and then the filename.

For example:

MYFILE.DOC

C:\WORPROC\REPORTS\MAY25.TXT

A:\MYFILE.BAK

Browsing panels from two applications. In the Windows 3.1 application (above) *Folders* are called *Directories*.

The Explorer display

Basic steps

The Explorer window has the usual frame controls and menu bar. The main working area is split, with the *All Folders* structure, or Tree, on the left, and the file list, or *Contents*, on the right.

The All Folders may show the disk drives and first level of folders only, but folders can be expanded to show some or all of the sub-folders. (See *Expanding folders*, overleaf.)

The Contents shows the files and sub-folders in the currently selected folder. These can be displayed as large or small icons accompanied by the name only, or with details of the file's size, type and date it was last modified. (See *Arranging icons*, page 62.)

The Status line shows the number of files in the folder, on the right, and the size of the selected files, on the left.

❑ Starting Explorer

1 Click [🔳 Start]

2 Point to Programs.

3 Click Explorer.

4 Click on a folder's icon 📁 or its name to open it 📂 and display its Contents.

Take note

The My Computer display is the same as that of Explorer, but without the All Folders pane. Its menu commands and Toolbar icons are identical.

③ Click Explorer

② Point to Programs

① Click Start

Basic steps

- ❑ Adding the Toolbar
- 1 Open the View menu
- 2 Click beside Toolbar to give it a checkmark.

- ❑ Icons and lists
- 1 Open the View menu.
- 2 Choose a display style.

or

- 1 Click the Toolbar icon.

Take note

The Toolbar icons are described on page 58.

View options

The View menu has several useful display options.

- ● If you prefer to work with icons rather than menu commands, turn on the Toolbar.

- ● You can switch between large and small icons, name-only and detailed lists to suit the job at hand.

① Open the View menu

② Turn the Toolbar on (or off)

② Pick a display style

All Folders   Contents   Toolbar

Drives
Root
First level folder
Current folder
Sub-folders
Status line

Expanding folders

The *All Folders* tree can be shown in outline form, or with some or all of its branches shown in full.

The best display is always the simplest that will show you all you need. In most cases, this means most of the tree is collapsed back to its first level of main folders, with one or two branches expanded to show particular sub-folders. Now and then it is worth expanding the whole tree, just to get an idea of the overall structure and to see how sub-folders fit together.

If a folder has sub-folders, it will have a symbol beside it.

⊞   has sub-folders, and can be expanded.

⊟   sub-folders displayed and can be collapsed.

❏ To expand a folder
1 Click the ⊞ by its name.

2 Click the ⊞ by any sub-folders if you want to fully expand the whole branching set.

❏ To collapse a folder
3 Click the ⊟ by its name.

❏ To collapse a whole branch
4 Click the ⊟ by the folder at the top of the branched set .

① Expand folder

④ Collapse whole set

③ Collapse folder

② Expand sub-folder

Basic steps

1 Point to the folder and click the right mouse button.

2 Select Properties from the short menu.

3 Wait for for the system to work out the total space and number of files.

4 Click ☒ to close the Properties panel.

Folder properties

Expanding a folder will show you what is in it, but not how much space all its files and folders occupy. The space report in the Status bar tells you how much is used by the files in the current folder only – not in its sub-folders. The total space figure can be important if you want to backup the folder, or copy it to floppies.

The Properties panel will tell us this – and other things.

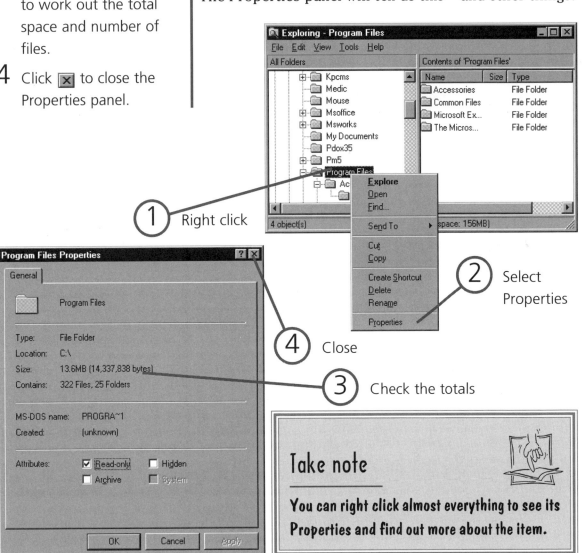

① Right click

② Select Properties

④ Close

③ Check the totals

Take note

You can right click almost everything to see its Properties and find out more about the item.

Creating a folder

Organized people set up their folders before they need them, so that they have places to store their letters – private and business, reports, memos, notes, and whatever, when they start to write them on their new system. They have a clear idea of the tree structure that they want, and create their folders at the right branches.

1 Select the folder that will be the parent of your new one, or the root if you want a new first level folder.

2 Open the File menu and point to New then select Folder.

3 Open the File menu and select Rename.

or

3 Click on the name twice – *separately.*

4 Replace "New Folder" with a new name – any length, any characters as with filenames.

① Click on the parent

② Select File–New–Folder

③ Select File–Rename

④ Edit the name

54

Basic steps

Moving folders

1 Arrange the display so that you can see the folder you want to move and the place it has to move to.

2 Drag the folder to its new position, *making sure the target is highlighted.*

Those of us who are less organized set up our new folders when the old ones get so full that it is difficult to find things. Nor do we always create them in the most suitable place in the tree. Fortunately, Windows 95 caters for us too. Files can easily be moved from one folder to another (See *Moving and copying*, page 66), and folders can easily be moved to new places on the tree.

In this example, *Cashflow* is being moved to its proper place as a branch of the *Excel* folder.

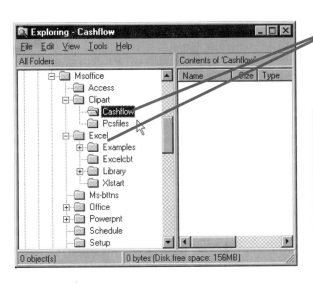

① Can you see the folder and its target?

② Drag to the target

Tip

Moving a folder – and all its files – to another disk can be a quick way to make a backup of a set of files.

Tip

If you can't get the original and target folders in the same display, use a multiple display. See page 67.

55

Deleting folders

This is not something you will do every day, for deleting a folder also deletes its files, and files are usually precious things. But there are times... We all acquire programs we don't need, keep files long past their use-by dates, and sometimes create unnecessary folders.

● Don't worry about accidental deletions – files and folders deleted from your hard disk can be restored thanks to the Recycle Bin. (See opposite.)

Use File–Delete

Select the folder

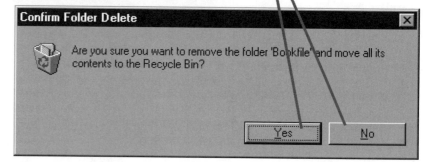

Confirm or stop

1 Select the folder – and check the files list. Are there any files? Do you want any of them? No, carry on.

2 Press [Delete] or select Delete from the File menu.

3 If necessary, you can stop the process by clicking No when you are asked to confirm that the folder is to be thrown in the bin.

Basic steps

The Recycle Bin

1 Double click the Recycle Bin icon on the main desktop.

2 Select the files that were in the deleted folder – the Original Location field shows you where they were.

3 Open the File menu and select Restore.

❑ The folder will be recreated and the files put back into it.

This is a wonderful feature, especially for those of us given to making instant decisions that we later regret. In Windows 95, deletions (from the hard disk) are done in two stages. The first stage is to throw the folder or file into the Recycle Bin. The second stage is to empty the bin – and until you empty it, anything in the bin can be instantly restored.

② Select the files

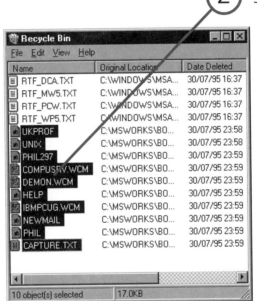

③ Use File–Restore

Take note

The Recycle Bin should be emptied regularly, to free up disk space. Check that there is nothing that you want then use File – Empty Recycle Bin.

Tip

If you don't know how to select groups of files, you can find out on page 64.

57

My Computer

At its default settings, the display of My Computer is simple, uncluttered and quite effective. You can see at a glance what files and folders are in the current folder – as long as there aren't too many! But sometimes, you need more control and more information.

Turn the Toolbar on, and you have instant access to some useful tools, plus a (limited) means of changing folders. The folder list on the Toolbar only shows the drives and the folders in the path from the root to the current one.

Switch to other drives or folders higher up the same path

	Go to parent folder
	Map networked drives
	Disconnect from network
	Cut – move folder or file to the Clipboard
	Copy file or folder to the Clipboard
	Paste from Clipboard into current folder
	Undo last action
	Delete file or folder
	Display properties of file or folder
	Large icon file display
	Small icon display
	Name only file list
	Detailed file list

Tip

The display can be adjusted in a number of ways – see Arranging icons, page 62.

Single window browsing

The main catch with the defaults is that each time you go into a new folder, it opens another window. This is useful if you want to open two folders, that both branch off from a previous one, so that you can move files from one to the other. It can be a nuisance, however, if you want to travel down the line to a third or fourth level folder. The screen clogs up with unwanted windows.

① Choose View Options

② Select single window

Basic steps

1 Open the View menu and select Options.

2 On the Folder panel, switch to Browse with single window.

Tip

If you hold [Ctrl] when you click on a folder, it is opened in the same window.

Summary

❏ You can use either Explorer or My Computer for managing your files and folders.

❏ The Toolbar gives you quick access to all the commonly used commands.

❏ Disks are normally subdivided into folders, to give organized storage for files.

❏ A folder's place in the tree is identified by its path.

❏ A filename has two components, the name itself and an extension.

❏ The name can be as long as you like, and contain any mixture of letters, digits and symbols.

❏ Extensions are used to identify the nature of the file.

❏ When you create a new folder, it will be placed on the branch below the selected folder.

❏ A folder, and its files, can be moved to a new position on the tree.

❏ A folder, and its files and sub-folders, can be deleted – but can be restored from the Recycle Bin if necessary.

❏ My Computer can be set to run in a single or multiple windows.

6 Managing files

Arranging icons

Unless you specify otherwise, the Contents display lists your folders and files in alphabetical order – icons arranged across the screen; lists arranged in columns. Most of the time this works fine, but when you are moving or copying files, or hunting for them, other arrangements can be more convenient.

Basic steps

1 Open the View menu and point to Arrange icons

2 Select by Name, Type, Size or Date.

3 If it is the size or date that you are interested in, click ▦ or use View – Details to get the full display.

Open View – Arrange icons

Select the sort order

Use the Details display with Size or Date lists

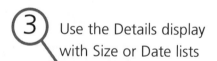

Tip

If you need to free up some disk space and are looking for files to delete, use the Details display and arrange the icons by size or by Date – the biggest and oldest are at the end of the lists.

Basic steps

❑ Adjusting Details

1 Point the cursor at the dividing line between two field headings.

2 When the cursor changes to ↔, drag the dividing line to change the width of the field on its left.

❑ Adjusting the split

3 Point anywhere on the bar between the panes to get the ↔ cursor.

4 Drag the shadowed line to adjust the relative size of the panes.

Improving visibility

The amount of information in a My Computer or Explorer Contents display can vary greatly, depending upon the number of items in a folder and the display style. It is important that you should be able to adjust the display so that you can see things properly.

As well as being able to adjust the overall size of the window, you can also adjust the width of each field in a Details display, and the split between the All Folders and Contents panes of Explorer.

① Get the cursor

② Drag the line

③ Get the cursor

④ Drag the line

Selecting sets of files

You can easily select single files by clicking on them, but you can also select groups of files. This is useful when you want to backup a day's work by copying the new files to a floppy disk, or move a group from one folder to another, or delete a load of files that are not wanted.

You can select:

- a block of adjacent files;
- a scattered set;
- the whole folder-full.

The same techniques work in Explorer and My Computer, with all display styles.

❑ To select a block using the mouse

1 Point to one corner of the block.

2 Drag an outline around the ones you want.

❑ [Shift] selecting

1 Click on the file at one end of the block.

2 If necessary, scroll the window to bring the other end into view.

3 Hold [Shift] and click on the far end file.

❑ You can reselect the far end file to redefine the block.

(1) Press the mouse button

(2) Drag to enclose

(1) Click

(2) Hold [Shift]

(3) Click

Basic steps

❏ To select scattered files

1 Click on any one of the files you want.

2 Hold [Ctrl] and click each of the other files.

❏ You can deselect any file by clicking on it a second time.

❏ To select all the files

1 Open the Edit menu.

2 Choose Select All.

① Select one file

② [Ctrl] click the rest

Tip

It may be easier to arrange icons by Name, Date or Type, and [Shift] select.

① Open the Edit menu

② Choose Select All

Tip

If you want all the files except for a scattered few, select them, then use Edit – Invert Selection to deselect them and select the others.

65

Moving and copying

When you drag a file from one place to another, it will either move or copy the file.

It is a move if you drag to somewhere *on the same disk.*

It is a copy if you drag the file *to a different disk.*

This is generally right. When you are dragging files within a disk, you are usually moving to reorganize your storage; and copying is most commonly done to create a safe backup on a separate disk.

❑ Moving within a disk

1 Select the file(s).

2 Scroll the All files list so that you can see the destination folder – the Contents display will stay the same as long as you don't click on the destination.

3 Point to one of the selected files and drag to the destination.

❑ Copying to a floppy

Either

1 Follow the steps for moving, but drag the files to a floppy drive.

or

1 Select the files.

2 Open the File menu, point to Send To and select the target drive.

① Select the file(s)

② Scroll to see the folder or drive

③ Drag the outline

② Send the file to a floppy

Basic steps

1 Open two Explorer or My Computer windows with one at the source and one at the destination folder.

2 Select the file(s).

3 Drag the files to their destination

Multiple windows

If you want to copy to a folder on a floppy, or you are having difficulty arranging the Explorer display so that you can see the source files and the target folder, the simplest approach is to use multiple windows. Use either Explorer or My Computer, or one of each.

① Open two windows

③ Drag across the desktop ② Select the files

Basic steps

1 Select the file(s).

2 *Move* with Edit – Cut.
   or
2 *Copy* with Edit – Copy.

3 Go to the destination drive or folder.

4 Give the Edit – Paste command.

Using the Clipboard

Windows 95 allows you to move and copy files and folders, as well as text, graphics and other data, through an area of memory called the Clipboard.

The Cut, Copy and Paste commands are on the Edit menu of all Windows applications. Use them to copy within a disk, or move files to another disk – or for all your copying and moving, if you don't like dragging.

Special moves

For those times when you do want to copy within a disk or move to another, Windows 95 provides a special technique.

If you hold the *right* button down while you drag, a menu opens when the file reaches its destination.

1 Set up Explorer or My Computer windows so that you can see the source and destination folders.

2 Select the file(s).

3 Hold down the right button and drag the files across.

4 Select Move or Copy from the menu.

① Set up the windows

② Select the file(s)

③ Hold the right button and drag

④ Move or Copy?

Take note

Files can be renamed in the same way as folders. See page 54.

68

Basic steps

1 Select the file, or group of files.

2 Press [Delete].

3 At the Confirm prompt, click Yes or No to confirm or stop the deletion.

Deleting files

Thanks to the Recycle Bin, deleting files is no longer the dangerous occupation that it used to be – up to a point! Anything that you delete from the hard disk goes first into the bin, from which it can easily be recovered. Floppies are different. If you delete a file from a floppy it really does get wiped out, and the only way you might be able to recover it is by using the MS-DOS Undelete program.

① Select the files

② Press [Delete]

③ Confirm

Take note

Restoring files from the Recycle Bin is covered on page 57.

Tip

Undelete works best if you exit to DOS and run it from there.

Finding files

If you are well organized, have a clear and logical structure of folders and store your files in their proper places, then you should rarely need this facility, except when hunting outside your system. However, if you belong to the other 90% of users, you will be grateful for this.

- Find can track down files by name, type, age, size or contents. As long as you have something to go on, no files need remain lost for long.

- You can run Find either from Explorer or from the Start menu.

Use either Tools – Find ...

Tools
| |
Find ► | **Files or Folders...**
Map Network Drive... | Computer...
Disconnect Network Drive... | On The Microsoft Network...
|
Go to...

① ... or Start – Find

② Select Files or Folders

Take note

The other Find options lead to different panels —to find a Computer on a network, or a service on the Microsoft Network

Partial names and Wildcards

If you just type part of a name into the Named slot, Find will track down any file with those characters anywhere in the name.

e.g. "DOC" will find "My Documents", "Letter to doctor", and all Word files with a .DOC extension.

If you know the start of the name and the extension, fill the gap with the wildcard *. (include the dot!)

e.g. "REP*.TXT" will find "REPORT MAY 15.TXT", "REPLY TO IRS.TXT" and similar files.

3 Type as much of the
  name as you know into
  the Named slot.

4 Select the drive from the
  Look in list or click
  [Browse..] if you want
  to restrict the search to
  a particular folder.

5 Click [Find Now]

6 If the file you want is
  not in the list, try one of
  the other methods (see
  next page).

  If it is there...

Either

7 Double click the file to
  run it, or open it with its
  associated program.

or

8 Click to select it and pull
  down the File menu.
  This has most of the
  Explorer filing options
  on it, and also allows
  you to open the file's
  folder.

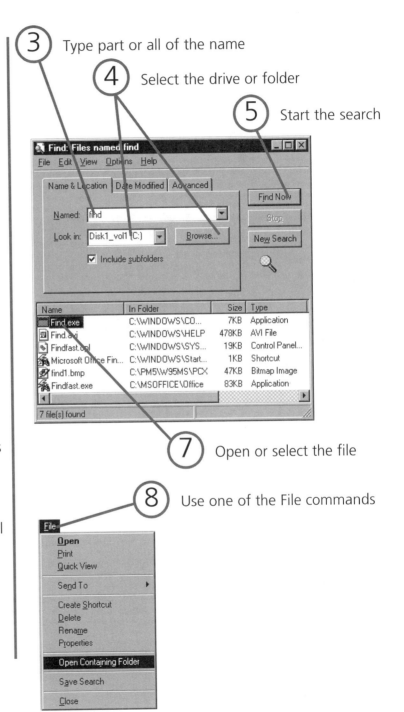

(3) Type part or all of the name

(4) Select the drive or folder

(5) Start the search

(7) Open or select the file

(8) Use one of the File commands

Finding by date

If you know when you last created or edited the file, but not its name, use the Date Modified tab to set the between limits or a previous days or months limit.

① Open the Date panel

② Choose the type

③ Set the limits

Basic steps

1 Click the Date Modified tab to open the panel.

2 Select the type of search – between, months or days.

3 Set the limits.

4 Start the search or go to another panel.

Tip

When finding by date, restrict the search to a selected folder or by setting Advanced criteria, to reduce the number of files in the output list.

Advanced searches

You can focus the search by specifying the File type, or a minimum or maximum size. With text files, you can also give a key word or phrase.

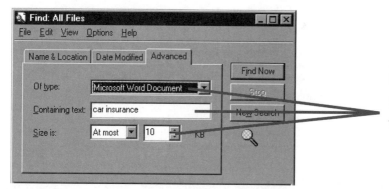

Specifying one or more of these helps to focus the search

Basic steps

1 Open the View menu.
2 Select Options.
3 Click the tab to open the View panel.
4 Select Show all files.
5 Click [OK]

The normal display does not necessarily show every file that is in a folder, for there are some types that you do not usually need to see and which are safer out of the way.

● Application extensions – files with .DLL extensions. They add extra features to applications.

● System files – marked by .SYS after the name. These are essential to Windows 95's internal workings.

● Drivers – with .VXD, .386 or .DRV extensions. These are the files that make printers, screens, mice and other hardware work properly.

The WINDOWS and WINDOWS/SYSTEM folders are full of them. You can see them by changing the View Options.

Take note

If you remove an application or change part of your hardware, you might want to delete the related DLL or driver files – in which case, you must be able to see them. But don't delete any file unless you are certain it is no longer needed.

73

Summary

❑ You can arrange icons by Name, Type, Size or Date.

❑ Files and folders can be displayed as icons or in lists with details.

❑ You can use [Shift] to select a block of files, or [Ctrl] to select a scattered set. A block of files can also be selected with the mouse.

❑ Dragging a file will normally move it within the disk, or copy it to a floppy.

❑ By holding the right button as you drag, you can copy within a disk or move to a floppy.

❑ To delete a file, press [Delete]. If the file was on the hard disk, it is sent to the Recycle Bin, from which it can be recovered.

❑ The Find utility will help you to track down files if you have forgotten where you put them, or what they were called.

❑ Those files that are essential to the system are usually hidden from view. They can be brought into view, but should always be treated with respect.

7 Programs and files

Properties

As we saw on page 21, everything in Windows 95 has Properties. If you open the Properties box for any file, you will see a General panel, containing information about the file and some controls. Some files have additional panels.

- Program files have Version panels carrying product details.

- Word-processor, spreadsheet and other data files created by newer applications have Summary and Statistics panels. Summary information is created by the application's user to describe the contents of the file; the Statistics include the number of pages, words, characters and the like, and the dates when the file was created, last modified or accessed.

- Shortcuts have their own special panels (see next pages).

Basic steps

1 Select the file and click the ☐ Tool.

or

1 Right click the file and select Properties from the short menu.

2 If you want to prevent the file from being edited, check the Read Only checkbox.

3 Click tabs to open other panels, if present.

4 Click OK or ☒ to close.

① Open the Properties box

② Protect from changes?

The Archive attribute is used by backup programs – it's best left alone

④ Click OK

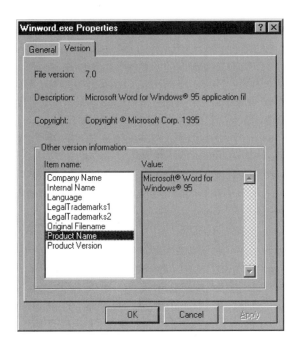

The Version panel (left) can tell you more about when and by whom a program was created. As its name implies, it is particularly useful for checking which version of a program you have.

The Summary panel (below) displays information written into it while the file was open in its application.

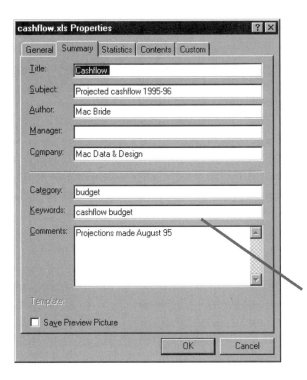

The file's Properties box displayed from Explorer

The file's Properties box opened for editing in Excel

Shortcuts

You can run a program by double-clicking on its EXE file in Explorer or My Computer, but Shortcuts make it easier. Shortcuts can be added to the Start menu (see page 106) or placed directly on the desktop. This is a very convenient way of running programs that you use regularly.

You can set up a shortcut in less than a minute – and if you find that you are not really making much use of it, you can remove a shortcut even faster!

Locate the program file

Select Create Shortcut

1 Use Explorer or My Computer to find the program file – it will have an EXE, or possibly COM extension.

2 Right click the file to open its short menu and select Create Shortcut.

3 If you are running Explorer Maximized, reduce it to Restore mode, so that you can see the desktop.

4 Find the new Shortcut icon in the program's folder.

5 Drag the Shortcut icon onto the desktop.

6 Edit the name to remove "Shortcut to..."

7 Open the icon's Properties box and click the Shortcut tab.

8 Change the Start in folder, Run mode or Icon as required.

Take note

Too many shortcuts will clutter up your Desktop.

Remove excess ones by selecting them and pressing [Delete]. This does not remove the program – only the shortcut.

③ Expose some Desktop

You can add shortcuts to your Start menu, see page 106.

Tip

④ Select the Shortcut icon

⑦ Open the Shortcut panel

⑤ Drag onto the Desktop

⑧ Edit if necessary

The folder where you normally store data files created by the application.

Maximized, Minimized or Normal window?

With an older MS-DOS program, you might want to change its icon.

79

File types

Windows 95 keeps a list of registered file types. These are ones that it knows how to describe and how to handle. If you double-click on, or open, a document of a known type, the system will run the appropriate application and load in the file. Windows 95 comes with a good long list, and you can teach it about new types through one of Explorer's View options.

1 Open the View menu and select Options...

2 Click the File Types tab to open its panel.

3 Click New Type...

4 Type in a Description.

5 Enter the Extension(s) that mark this type.

6 You must define the Actions that can be performed on this file. Click New...

7 In the Action slot, type "*open*".

8 Go to the application slot then Browse... through your folders and select it.

9 Close and OK back to the main panel.

① Select View Options

② Open the File Types panel

③ Click New Type

Tip

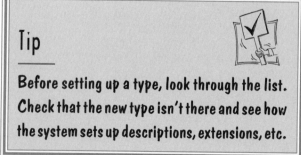

Before setting up a type, look through the list. Check that the new type isn't there and see how the system sets up descriptions, extensions, etc.

Add New File Type

Change Icon...

Description of type: Visual Basic code

④ Enter a Description

Associated extension: MAK

⑤ Give the extension(s)

Content Type (MIME):

Default Extension for Content Type:

Actions:

New... Edit... Remove Set Default

☐ Enable Quick View
☐ Always show extension

OK Cancel

⑥ Click New

Take note

Other common Actions are print and play – but open is the most important.

⑦ Type open

⑨ Click OK

New Action

Action:
open

OK

Cancel

Application used to perform action:
C:\sysquest\VB\Vb.exe

Browse...

☐ Use DDE

⑧ Browse for a program

Take note

If you know the full path and filename of the application that you want to use, you can type it in directly – but Browsing is sometimes quicker, and often more accurate!

Open With

Look in: Vb

Dispcalc.reg | Packing.lst | Rainbow.dib | Test.nte
External.txt | Pastel.dib | Readme.txt | Test1
Gates.frx | Payroll.dat | Slide.frm | Test2.nte
Note2a.nte | Perform.txt | Slide.mak | Vb.exe
Notes.nte | Phone03.ico | Staff.dta | Vb.hlp
Noteson.nte | Project1.mak | Student.dta

File name: Vb.exe

Open

Files of type:

Cancel

81

Open With...

The View Options File Type panel offers a thorough, if slightly long-winded, means of registering new types. A rough and ready alternative is to simply tell Windows what program to use as and when you try to open unknown types of files.

Unknown
file type

Select Open With...

Give a description

Select a
program

Browse for
a program

Always use this?

Click OK

- ❑ Opening With ...

1 Right click a file to get its short menu. If the first item is Open, no steps need be taken.

2 If the top item is Open With..., select it.

3 At the Open With dialog box, type a Description. This will be used in Details displays in Explorer.

4 Scroll through the list and pick the program to use with this file.

5 If you can't find the program in the list click   Other...   and browse through your folders to find it.

6 Check the Always use this program box, if wanted – sometimes you may want to use the same file with different programs.

7 Click   OK

Basic steps

Editing a type

1 Select the type.

2 Click [Edit...]

Either

3 Select an action and click [Edit...] to link a new program.

or

4 Change the icon.

or

5 Turn Quick View on or off.

Whether you set up your new type through the View Options, or through Open With, it is possible that it may need some fine tuning later. You may want to change its icon, or turn Quick View (see overleaf) on or off.

Established file types may also need editing over time as you replace programs with newer versions, but still retain the data files.

The Edit panel is reached through View Options.

① Select the type

② Click Edit

③ Edit an action

④ Change the icon

⑤ Quick View?

Tip

Sometimes it is quicker to remove a type definition and start from scratch, rather than to edit it.

Quick View

You will appreciate this facility if, like me, you cannot always identify a file by its name – time passes and we forget. As the name suggests, it gives a means of taking a quick look at a document. Typically it is three to four times faster to open a document in Quick View than in its original application.

Not all document files will work with Quick View, but you can view any Microsoft Office spreadsheet, presentation, database or Word file, bitmaps, more or less any text file, and some others. It seems to cover documents from most of the big, new applications – the ones that take so long to load – and those are the ones that matter most.

Basic steps

1 Locate the file with Explorer or My Computer.

2 Right click to open the short menu.

3 If Quick View is present, select it.

4 Click the program icon or select Open File for Editing from the short menu if you want to work on it.

③ Select Quick View

Icon of the file's original program

④ Edit the file?

Enlarge or reduce the font size

84

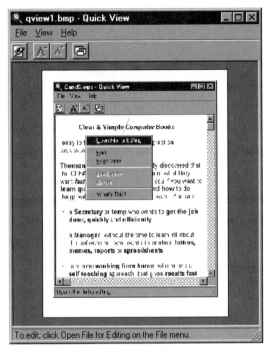

Quick View options

As well as Open File for Editing, the short menu offers:

Page view – probably the most useful;

Landscape – shows how the document would fit on paper, if turned sideways;

Rotate – turns the document through a quarter circle (Why?!);

Font – lets you choose the style and size of text.

Take note

Once Quick View is open, you can drag other files onto it for viewing.

Drag in to replace the current document

Summary

❑ The Properties box of a file can be a useful source of information.

❑ You can create Shortcuts to programs and place them on your desktop for quick and easy access.

❑ If Windows 95 knows about a file type, it knows how to describe it and what program to open it with. You can teach the system about new types.

❑ When you try to open a file of an unknown type, you will get the Open With option and can then tell it which program to use.

❑ The Quick View utility can be a convenient way of checking through your documents.

8 Disk housekeeping

The System Tools

Windows 95 comes equipped with a set of disk housekeeping tools – programs that help to keep your disks in good condition, and your data safe.

Scandisk – finds and fixes errors in data stored on disks.

Defrag – optimises the disk's speed and efficiency.

Backup – provides a means of creating safe and compact backup copies of your files.

Drivespace – allows you to double the capacity of disks.

Inbox Repair tool – fixes any errors in your mail files.

Resource Meter – runs minimized in the background. Right click on its icon on the Taskbar, to see what percentages of your system's resources are in use.

System Monitor – lets you examine the performance of different aspects of the system.

Basic steps

1 Click ▓Start

2 Point to Programs.

3 Point to Accessories.

4 Point to System Tools.

5 Click to select a tool.

④ System Tools

⑤ Pick a tool

③ Accessories

② Programs

① Click Start

88

Basic steps

Routine chores

1 Open My Computer and right click on the drive you want to work on.

2 Bring the Tools tab to the front.

3 Select a tool.

The three system tools that are needed for the routine housekeeping chores can also be reached from the Properties box of any disk. The messages will remind you of chores you have been neglecting!

① Right click on C:

② Open the Tools panel

This is Scandisk

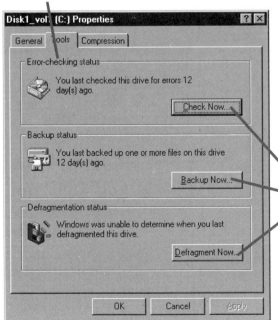

③ Pick a tool

Scandisk

Data is stored on disks in *allocation units*. A small file may fit on a single unit, but others are spread over many. A file's units may be in a continuous run or scattered over the disk (see *Disk Defragmenter,* page 96), but are kept together by links from one to the next. Sometimes these links get corrupted leaving *Lost fragments*, with no known links to any file, or *Cross-linked files*, where two are chained to the same unit of data. Scandisk can find – and often fix – these problems.

Sometimes the magnetic surface of the disk becomes corrupted, creating *Bad sectors* where data cannot be stored safely. Scandisk can identify these and, with a bit of luck, retrieve any data written there and transfer it to a safe part of the disk.

1 Run Scandisk from the Start menu or the disk's Properties box.

2 Select the Drive to be scanned.

3 Normally go for the quicker Standard scan, to fix file errors only. Do a Thorough scan to check for bad sectors on new disks and then every couple of months.

4 Set Advanced options as required – see opposite.

5 Click ▐ Start ▌

② Select a drive ③ Standard or Thorough?

④ Open the Advanced box

⑤ Start it off

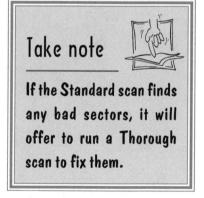

Take note

If the Standard scan finds any bad sectors, it will offer to run a Thorough scan to fix them.

Advanced options

The *Summary* is always worth having.

Turn off the *log* if you don't use it.

Lost file fragments *Convert to files* only works with text. The new files are called CHKDSK.001 and similar. You may be able to recover some of your text from the fragments.

Free up the space if your files are mainly graphics, spreadsheets or databases. You won't be able to recover anything useful from the fragments.

Cross-linked files *Make copies* is generally worth trying – one of the two files may still work.

Check host drive first Only relevant where Drivespace is used. (See page 98).

Invalid dates are rare but can cause problems with backups.

Scandisk has found bad sectors on this floppy. It has also prevented future errors by marking them off so that they are not used.

The available storage units number is slightly less than the total as a few units are needed for the disk's index.

Backup

Modern hard disks are very reliable, but they can all develop problems eventually – some sooner than others. Making safe backup copies of your documents should be part of your regular routines.

- Do a full backup of the C: drive after installing Windows 95, and again later after any major changes.

- Backup your document files after you have done a substantial amount of work – this may mean every day, or once a month, depending upon your activity.

With partial backups, you should filter out all the irrelevant files – exclude every type except those of documents that you have created.

④ Select All then deselect the ones you want

You can delete types from the Exclude list if you need to

⑤ Click Exclude, then OK

1 Run Backup from the Start menu or the disk's Properties box.

2 For a Full backup, select Drive C: and jump to step 7.

3 Open the Settings menu and select File Filtering.

4 In the File Types, click Select All, then work through the list and deselect your document types.

5 Click Exclude then OK to return to the main dialog box.

6 Select single files or whole folders of files to be backed up.

7 Click Next Step >

8 Select the Device– and folder if appropriate – to hold the backup.

9 Click Start Backup

10 Give a name for the backup file.

Selection symbols

Folders

☑ Some files selected

☑ All files selected

Files

☑ This one selected

③ Use Settings –
File Filtering

⑦ Click Next Step

⑥ Select files or folders
to back up

⑧ Select the device

⑨ Start the backup

⑩ Name the backup set

Tip

Tape storage devices for backing up are cheap, reliable and much easier to handle than piles of floppies!

Backup options

Do make sure that data compression is turned on. This almost always saves space – though the backup control information adds an overhead, so that the backup of a single file may be larger than the original!

Some types of files can be compressed more than others. Typical space-savings:

  Programs 25%; Text files 33%; Graphics 75%

Take note

If you want to backup the same set of files regularly, save the set definition with the command File – Save As. Next time you want to backup the same files, use File – Open File Set to load in the definition.

Saves having to close down Backup after it has done

Use *Full* the first time you save a set of files

Use *Incremental* for later backups of the same set

Turn this on!

Turn on verification if you have any doubts about the quality of your backup tapes/disks

Automatic formatting is a convenience for tape users

Only set the Always erase options if you are confident you will not try to save over a backup file that you want

Basic steps

1 Run Backup and click the Restore tab to open its panel.

2 Select the Device, then the Backup set.

3 Click Next Step.

4 Pick the files you want to restore.

5 Click Start Restore.

With any luck, you will never have to restore a lost file. However, should you need to, it's a simple process.

① Open the Restore panel

③ Click Next Step

② Select device and file

④ Select the files

⑤ Start the Restore

Tip

If you want to check that the backup is accurate, use the Compare panel. The steps are almost identical to Restore.

Disk Defragmenter

When you first start to write data onto a disk, the files go on, one after the other, with each occupying a continuous run of disk space. When you access one of these files, the drive simply finds the start point, then reads the data in a single sweep.

After the disk has been in use for some time, holes begin to appear in the layout, and not all files are stored in a continuous area. Some have been deleted, others will have grown during editing, so that they no longer fit in their original slot, but now have parts stored elsewhere on the disk. When you store a new file, there may not be a single space large enough for it, and it is stored in scattered sections.

The drive is becoming *fragmented*. The data is still safe, but the access speed will suffer as the drive now has to hunt for each fragment of the file.

Basic steps

1 Run the Defragmenter from the Start menu or the disk's Properties box.

2 Select the drive.

3 Check the status.

4 If the fragmentation is over 10%, click Start

   Under 5%, click Exit

   In between, do it if you have spare time.

5 When defragmenting starts, click Show Details to see what's going on.

6 Go for a coffee – it can take up to an hour to defragment a large drive.

② Select a drive

③ Check the state

④ Start or Exit

Tip

Run the Defragmenter regularly to keep your drives running at their top speed. The half hour or so it takes will save time in the long run.

⑤ Show Details to see it at work

The Legend shows what the colored squares mean

Watching the Defragmenter at work is more exciting than watching paint dry, but not much more.

Advanced options

The defaults are usually right. Change them only if essential.

Improves access times on existing files, but new files may be scattered.

New files will be stored efficiently, but existing ones remain fragmented.

Check if you haven't run Scandisk recently.

DriveSpace

It seems that every new version of every application that comes along takes up more disk space than the last. Only a few years ago a 40Mb hard disk would have more than enough capacity for most people, but now even a 500Mb disk soon fills up. It's just as well that DriveSpace is around. This stores files in a compressed form and can almost double the capacity of a disk.

You can compress floppy disks, boosting their capacity to around 2.6Mb. This is certainly worth doing if you backup onto floppies.

Installing it on your hard disk is a slow process, but you only have to do it once!

1 Run DriveSpace.

2 Select the disk to be compressed.

3 Open the Drive menu and select Compress.

4 You will see an estimate of the space gain. The actual gain will depend upon the types of files on your disk, as some can be compressed more than others. If the gain is worthwhile – and it should be – click

> Start

3 Use Drive – Compress

2 Select a drive

4 Click Start

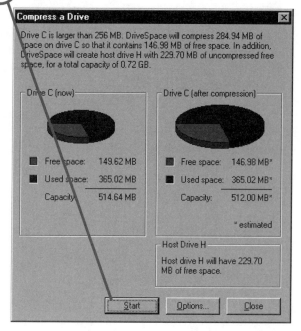

Take note

You can also run DriveSpace from the Compression panel of a drive's Properties box.

98

5 If you have not backed up the disk recently, take the offer to do so now – there's a very slight possibility that files could get corrupted.

6 Click [Compress Now] and put your feet up for a while.

5 Backup if you need to

6 Start the process

DriveSpace3

DriveSpace2 is limited to 512Mb in the size of compressed drives it can create – using about 250Mb of uncompressed drive. If wanted, any remaining uncompressed space can be made into a second drive.

DriveSpace3, part of the Microsoft Plus! package, has no such limit – it can compress drives of any size. It can also compress them more tightly! Compare its report, here, with that of DriveSpace 2, opposite.

Formatting a floppy

Before you can use a new floppy disk, it must beformatted. This marks out magnetic tracks on the disk surface, dividing the area up into numbered blocks to provide organized storage space.

The Format command takes the hard work out of this – all you have to do is make sure that you know what kind of disk you are formatting.

PC disks come in two sizes and four capacities.

    5.25 inch   360Kb Double-Density (DD)

    5.25 inch   1.2Mb High-Density (HD)

    3.5 inch   720Kb Double-Density (DD)

    3.5 inch   1.44Mb High-Density (HD)

PCs are normally fitted with 3.5 inch drives, that can take either capacity. The 1.44Mb disk gives you better value for your money.

1 Insert the disk into the drive.

2 Run My Computer or Explorer.

3 Open the Properties menu and select Format.

4 At the dialog box, make sure that it is set for the right disk size.

5 Select Full.

6 Click [Start]

② Run My Computer

③ Select Format

④ Check the Capacity

⑥ Start

This clears files off used floppies

⑤ Use Full

Labels are optional – they can help to identify disks

Caring for floppies

Disk drives can be mounted horizontally or vertically, but a disk will only go in one way. If it won't fit, don't force it. Try it the other way.

The modern 3.5 inch floppy is a far tougher beast than the older 5.25 inch ones. Its plastic casing protects it well against grime, knocks and splashes of coffee, but it still has enemies. Heat, damp and magnetism will both go through the casing and corrupt the data on the disk beneath. So, keep your disks away from radiators, sunny windowsills, magnets, heavy electrical machinery or mains cables – these last two produce magnetic fields.

Up

Activity light   Eject button

Shutter   Disk surface

This side up and this way in

Write protect hole

2nd hole, only on HD disks

Tip

Move the slider at the back of the disk to open the write-protect hole, if you want to prevent files from being deleted or changed.

Summary

- Windows 95 is supplied with a set of very useful system tools.

- Scandisk can find and fix errors on your disks.

- Backup provides a simple and efficient way of creating backup copies of your files. The backups are compressed, significantly saving space.

- If you lose backed up files, they can be recovered using Restore.

- The Disk Defragmenter should be run regularly to ensure that files are stored compactly, and can therefore be loaded faster.

- DriveSpace can more or less double the effective capacity of a floppy or hard disk.

- DriveSpace3, part of the Microsoft Plus set, can handle very large hard disks.

- Floppy disks must be fully formatted before they can be used.

- If you want to reuse a disk with old files on it, the Quick Format option is the fastest way to erase files.

- Floppies should be stored safely away from heat, damp and sources of magnetism.

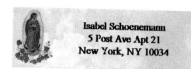

Isabel Schoenemann
5 Post Ave Apt 21
New York, NY 10034

9 The Taskbar

Taskbar options

Many parts of the Windows 95 system can be tailored to your own needs and tastes. Some of the most important are covered in the next three sections. We'll start with the Taskbar and the Start menu.

You can adjust the size of the Taskbar icons, turn the clock on or off, hide the Taskbar, or place it on any edge of the screen.

❑ Adjusting the display

1 Click **Start**

2 Point to Settings.

3 Click on Taskbar.

4 Turn an option on or off.

5 Click **Apply** to see how it looks.

6 Repeat for other options until you have it as you want it.

7 Click **OK** to fix the settings and close.

② Point to Settings

③ Click on Taskbar

① Start here

④ Toggle an option

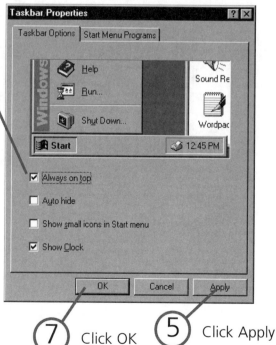

⑦ Click OK   ⑤ Click Apply

Always on Top – when turned off, you can make the Taskbar visible by minimizing your applications, or by pressing [Ctrl]-[Esc].

Auto-Hide reduces the Taskbar to a thin line at the bottom of the screen. Pointing at it restores it to size.

104

Basic steps

Moving and resizing

□ Moving

1 Point to any free space on the Taskbar.

2 Drag towards the top, left or right of the screen, as desired.

3 Release the mouse button.

□ Resizing

1 Point to the inner edge of the Taskbar.

2 When the cursor changes to ↔, drag to change the size of the Taskbar.

Moving the Taskbar is quite easy to do by mistake, so it is just as well to know how to do it intentionally – if only to correct a mistake!

Resizing the Taskbar – making it deeper, or wider – is sometimes useful. Narrow vertical displays are almost unreadable.

When you are running a lot of programs with a horizontal Taskbar, the titles on the buttons can be very small. If you deepen the display, you get two rows of decent sized buttons.

Take note

Unless you have a lot of applications running at once, horizontal displays make far better use of screen space.

② Drag to resize

② Drag into place

① Point to a clear part

The Start menu

When Windows 95 was installed onto your system, it created a Start menu that included shortcuts to all its own applications and accessories, plus any others that it found on your system. If you had been running Windows 3.1, it will have taken your Program Manager groups and incorporated them into the Start menu structure. When you install new software onto your system at a later date, the installation routine should also bring them into the Start menu.

If it gets built automatically, why would we want to mess around with it? The answer is that installation routines can only do so much. They may not structure the menus as you would like. Also, not all software comes with a routine to install it into Windows 95.

The Start Menu Programs panel of the Taskbar Properties box gives you control of your menu structure.

Take note

The Start menu is a folder in the Windows folder. Its sub-menus are sub-folders and the entries are shortcuts in those folders. You can manage your Start menu by adding, deleting or moving files and folders through Explorer – but the buttons on the Properties panel make all these jobs easier.

Use these buttons to change the entries on your menus

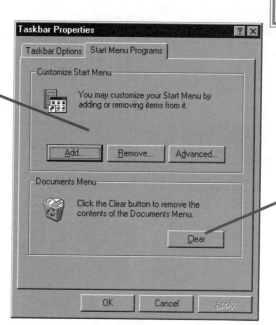

Click here if you ever want to remove all the Documents entries from the Start menu

Basic steps

1 Click [Add...]

2 Click [Browse...] and work through your folders to find and select the program.

3 Select the menu folder to hold the new entry.

4 Replace the program's filename with a more meaningful name.

Adding entries

You can add individually any programs that were not handled by the installation routines. All that is essential is that you know where to find them.

Type the path and filename if you like

(2) Browse for the file

(3) Pick the folder

(4) Rename the entry

Take note

Click Next after completing each panel, and Finish at the end. Use Back, if needed, to correct a mistake.

Organizing the menu

The Advanced button takes you into Explorer, with the focus on the Start menu folder. From here you can rename, reorganize, delete, create new shortcuts and move them into menu folders. The one job you are most likely to want to do is reorganize.

When you install modern software, you typically get not just one, but several programs – and several menu entries. As well as the application, there will often be a ReadMe First file, Help pages, an uninstall program, and perhaps a clutch of minor utilities. Most of these will be rarely used, and are little more than clutter on the menus.

Unwanted entries can be removed altogether (see page 110), or tucked into their own sub-menu.

(see page 110)

❑ Making a sub-menu

1 Click   Advanced...

2 Select the over-crowded folder.

3 Open the File menu and select New – Folder.

4 Rename the folder.

5 Select the excess entries and drag them onto the new folder.

6 Close Explorer.

Take note

Office 95 is a classic over-filler of menus. After installation, there are 18 entries in its menu! They are all useful, but some are not wanted often and would be better in a sub-menu.

108

③ Use File – New
  – Folder

② Select the folder

④ Rename the new
    folder

⑥ Close Explorer

⑤ Drag the files to the new folder

The revised menu is
much easier to use,
but the accessories
are still there if
needed.

109

Removing entries

If you remove software from your system, you will need to remove its entry from the Start menu. You may also want to remove entries for programs that are very rarely used – if necessary they can be added back onto the menu later, or run by double-clicking on them in Explorer.

Removing entries is even easier than adding new ones. But don't worry about deleting entries by mistake – like all deletions from the hard disk, the entries go first to the Recycle Bin.

1 Click Remove...

2 Open up sub-folders if necessary, until you can see the entry.

3 Select the entry.

4 Click Remove...

5 Repeat steps 2 to 4 as necessary to remove all unwanted entries.

6 Click Close to return to the Properties panel.

② Open folders as necessary

③ Select the entry

④ Click Remove

⑥ Close when done

Tip

If you send a whole folder to the Recycle Bin by mistake, it will be recreated if you restore one or more of its files.

Basic steps

Setting the Clock

1 Right click on the clock to open the short menu.

2 Select Adjust Date/Time.

3 Pick the Month from the drop down list.

4 Click on the Day.

5 Click on Hour, Minute or Second to select, then either adjust with the arrows or type the correct value.

6 Click [Apply] to restart the clock.

We can't leave the Taskbar without having a look at adjusting the Date and Time. This should not need doing often – PCs keep good time, and Windows 95 even puts the clock forward and back for Daylight Saving Time!

② Select Adjust Date/Time

③ Pick the month

④ Click on the day

⑤ Highlight then edit

⑥ Restart the clock

If you want to change the Time Zone, either pick the zone from the drop-down list, or click on the zone line and drag it left or right.

Summary

❏ The Taskbar can be reduced to a thin line or allowed to lie behind active windows, but is easiest to use if it is visible and always on top.

❏ The Taskbar can be moved to any edge of the screen, and resized if needed.

❏ The Start menu is a folder in the Windows folder. Its entries are folders or shortcuts to programs. It can be managed through Explorer or My Computer, but changes are simpler through the Settings.

❏ You can add new entries to the menu by creating shortcuts and storing them in a chosn folder.

❏ The menu can be reorganized by moving entries to new or other existing folders.

❏ Unwanted menu entries are easily removed.

❏ The Clock can be set by opening its short menu.

10 The Control Panel

The settings

The Control Panel allows you to customize many of the features of Windows to your own need and tastes.

Some settings are best left at the defaults set by Windows 95; some should be set when new hardware or software is added to the system; some should be set once then left alone; a few can be altered whenever you feel like a change.

Nine of those control settings that can or should be adjusted are covered in this section.

Basic steps

1 Click Start.

2 Point to Settings.

3 Select Control Panel.

Either

4 Right click an icon and Open it from the short menu.

or

4 Double click on an icon.

② Point to Settings

③ Select Control Panel

For Date/Time see Section 9

For Printers see Section 11

④ Open or double click

① Click Start

Take note

What's in your Control panel depends upon the hardware and software on your system.

114

Adjusting the keys

1 Click on the lines beside the pointers to adjust the Repeat Delay and Rate.

2 Click on the test area and hold down a key.

3 Repaet 1 and 2 until you are happy.

4 Adjust the Cursor blink rate to suit.

5 Click [OK] to fix the settings.

This is a small but significant adjustment. When you hold down a key, the system will – after a little while – start to repeat that key's character. This can be very useful if you want a line of dashes or asterisks across the screen.

The two questions are, how long is a little while, and how fast should the characters be repeated?

The answers depend entirely upon your touch. If you are a struggling two-finger typist, go for a Long Repeat Delay and a Slow Repeat Rate or you will find that you are regularly getting more out of the keyboard than you wanted.

After you have changed a setting, click on the Test slot and hold down a key. Do you have easily enough time to get your finger clear before it starts to repeat, and after the system has repeated enough characters?

Use the Language panel to set up for a second language

Only used after fitting a new keyboard

Click to change

Click and type to test

Adjust to suit

Click OK

The Display

Display

This may seem to be pure frills and fancies, but it does have a serious purpose. If you spend a lot of time in front of your screen, being able to see it clearly and use it comfortably is important.

Background panel

The Wallpaper is the background to the desktop. Some of the supplied designs are hideous, but others are acceptable. If you are artisitic, you can create your own with Paint, or scan a photo and save it as a bitmap (BMP) file.

With a large image, set it in the Center rather than duplicate it as a Tile.

If you prefer a single color background, you may want to impose a Pattern on it.

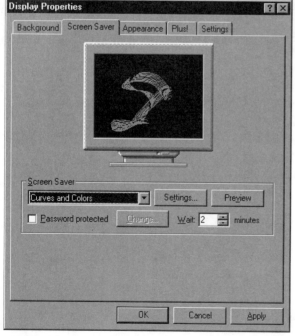

Screen Savers

These are fun but serve little real purpose nowadays. (On an old monitor, if a static image was left on too long, it could burn into the screen.) A screen saver switches to a moving image after the system has been left inactive for a few minutes.Preview the ones that are offered. Settings allows you to adjust the images.

There is a small industry churning out weird and wonderful screen savers for you to buy, if you want something different.

Appearance

This controls the color schemes and the size of fonts. There is a set of ready made schemes, or you can select individual parts of the screen from the Item list and adjust the Color or Font. The scheme can then be saved with a new name.

There are High Contrast and colored Large and Extra large (font) schemes if easy viewing is needed.

If you make a mess of the scheme – easily done! – restore the appearance by selecting the Windows Standard.

Settings

Play with the other panels as much as you like, but treat this one with respect. In particular, do not use Change Display Type unless you are unhappy with the current display *and* you know what you are doing. You can switch to a display mode that it not properly supported by your hardware, resulting in a screen which is difficult or impossible to read – and therefore to correct!

If you do produce an unreadable screen, reboot the system using the Startup disk – you did make one, didn't you – and restore the default setting from there.

Adjusting the mouse Basic steps

Mouse

The Double-click Speed determines the difference between a proper double click and two separate clicks.

Don't change to Left handed unless you are the only one who uses the system, and it is the only system that you use. You will only confuse yourself and others.

❏ Buttons panel

1 Set the Double-click speed.

2 Test it.

3 Click [Apply]

❏ Motion panel

4 Set the Pointer Speed.

5 Test it at the bottom of the panel.

6 Click [Apply].

① Adjust

② Test

③ Apply

④ Adjust

⑤ Test

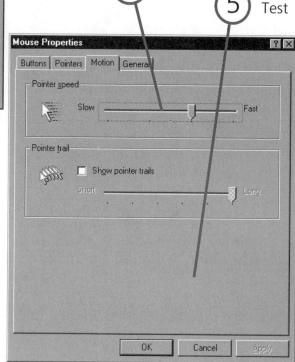

The Pointer Speed links speed and distance, so that the faster you move the mouse, the further the pointer goes. At the Fastest, a quick flick will take the pointer across the screen.

Pointer Trails make the mouse easier to see on LCD screens of portables.

Basic steps

Pointers

❑ Pointers panel

1 Pick a Scheme.

2 Select an action.

3 Click [Browse...]

4 Pick a cursor image for the action.

5 Click [Open]

6 Repeat steps 2 to 5 for any other actions.

7 Click [OK]

There are alternative Schemes, including ones with large and extra large pointers. You can also pick your own images (and animated ones with Microsoft Plus!) to link to chosen mouse actions.

Check out the Preview

Select an image

Tip

Find Pointer and Double-click speeds that suit you and *stick with them.* If you keep fiddling with these, you will never get the feel of the mouse.

Sounds

Sounds

Windows allows you to attach sounds to events. You may find this an effective way of alerting you to what's happening, or regard it as more noise pollution. It all depends upon your point of view. I like a fanfare when the system is ready to start work (to wake me up – well, you wait so long!) but very few other sounds. Try them out – the Utopia sounds are worth listening to.

Basic steps

1 Pick a Scheme.

2 Select an event.

3 Click ▶ to Preview its sound.

4 Sample a few more.

5 Go back to step 1 and try alternative schemes until you have found the one you like best.

6 To set individual sounds, Browse for an alternative, or select [none] for the Name.

7 Click [Apply] or [OK]

② Select an event

③ Preview its sound

⑥ Browse for a new sound

① Pick a Scheme

⑦ Click OK

Take note

With a sound card and speakers, the quality of sound compares well to a (cheap) HiFi system. If you are limited to the PC's own speaker, you don't get the same quality, but you can still hear sounds.

Regional
Settings

Regional settings

Basic steps

☐ Date styles

1 Run Regional Settings.

2 Open the Date panel

3 Pick a Short date style from the list and edit it to your taste.

4 Click [Apply]

5 Point to the Taskbar clock and see how it looks.

6 Repeat for the Long date.

These control the units of measurement and the styles used by most applications for displaying dates, time, currency and other numbers. The choice of Region in the top panel sets the defaults for the rest.

The other panels are for fine tuning the styles. The Date panel is a good example. There are Short date and Long date styles. Both use the same coding:

Day	Month	
d	M	Number
dd	MM	Number with leading 0 if needed
ddd	MMM	Three letter name
dddd	MMM	Full name
Year	yy for 95; yyyy for 1995	

② Open the Date panel

③ Pick a style and edit

⑥ Repeat

④ Apply it

Take note

Setting the clock is covered on page 111.

⑤ Check it out

To get this, the Long date style was edited to:
dddd d MMMM yyyy

Fonts

Fonts

There is one school of thought that says you can never have enough fonts. There is a decent core supplied with Windows itself, and you will normally acquire more with any word-processor and desktop publishing packages that you install. If these are not enough for you, there are whole disks full of fonts available commercially and through the shareware distributors. Check the ads in any PC magazine if you are interested.

Installing new fonts is quick and easy.

❑ Adding fonts

1 Place the disk of new fonts into a drive.

2 Open the File menu and select Install New Font.

3 At the dialog box, select the drive and folder.

4 Wait while the system reads the names of the fonts on the disk.

5 Click [Select All], or work through the list and select the ones you want to install.

6 Click [OK]

② Use File – Install New Font

④ Wait for the list

③ Set the drive and folder

⑥ Click OK

⑤ Select All or some

If the fonts are already in a folder on the C: drive, you don't need to copy the files.

Basic steps

Removing unwanted fonts

- ❏ Font samples
1 Select a font.
2 Select Open from the File menu or the short menu.
3 Click [Print] to see how it looks on paper.
4 Click [Done] to close the viewer.
5 If it is not useful, press [Delete] to remove it.

This is as easy as adding them and well worth doing. You will save space on the hard disk, speed up Windows' start up and have a shorter set to hunt through when you are setting a font in an application.

Open a font file, if you want a detailed sample of the font.

② Use File – Open

① Select a font

④ Click Done to close

③ Print a sample if wanted

Tip

There are sometimes subtle differences between the screen and printed appearance of fonts. Print a sample before you use a font for any extensive work.

Mail and Fax

Basic steps

What options you have here will depend upon whether or not you are on a local area network, have a modem and a connection to an external communications service.

Most of the properties of all of these will have been set during installation, and should not be altered. The main exception is the Fax, where you may want to set your own defaults.

1 Select Microsoft Fax.

2 Click Properties.

3 Set the transmission Time.

4 If your faxes are plain text, they will travel faster if you click Paper and select 200 x 100 dpi resolution.

5 Turn on the Cover page, if wanted, then select the default.

1 Pick Microsoft Fax

2 Click Properties

3 Set the Time

4 Set the resolution

5 Cover page?

Take note

These settings can be altered when you send faxes.

Basic steps

System

1 Open the Performance panel.

2 Click [File System...].

3 At the File System Properties box, open the CD-ROM panel.

4 Drop down the list at Optimize access pattern and select your type of CD-ROM.

5 Click [OK]

6 [Close] the main box.

Most of the options in this box fall into the *look but don't touch* category – any changes are best left to the system to handle for itself. There is one exception. You should check that it is optimized for your CD-ROM drive, if you have one.

(1) Open the Performance panel

(2) Click File System

(6) Close

(3) Open the CD-ROM panel

(4) Select your CD-ROM type

(5) Click OK

Summary

- ❑ The Control Panel contains routines that determine the settings of some of the most basic features of how Windows works.

- ❑ Adjust the mouse and keyboard responses to your own needs at an early stage, then leave them alone.

- ❑ The Display options give you plenty of scope for personal preferences. Set the wallpaper, patterns, color scheme and fonts to suit yourself – but don't change the main settings unless you have to.

- ❑ There are several mouse pointer schemes, and individual pointers can be redesigned.

- ❑ Sounds can be assigned to events, to alert you when things happen.

- ❑ The Regional settings control the appearance of dates, times, currency and numbers in most Windows applications.

- ❑ New Fonts can be installed easily. It is just as easy to examine fonts and to remove unnecessary ones.

- ❑ Communications with the outside world are controlled through the Mail and Fax settings.

- ❑ The core System settings should be mainly left to the system to manage. It knows what it's doing!

11 Printers

Printer settings

Windows 95 knows about printers, just as it knows about most other bits of hardware that you might attach to your system. If you installed 95 over Windows 3.1, it will have picked up the printer settings from there; if Windows 95 was your first operating system, the printer will have been set up during installation. Either way, as long as you continue to use the same printer, with the same settings, you shouldn't need to bother with the next four pages.

However, things change, and there are alternatives to some of the defaults that are worth exploring.

Basic steps

1 Click **Start**.

2 Point to Settings.

3 Select Printers.

4 Right click a printer to open its short menu.

5 Select Properties.

② Point to Settings

③ Select Printers

① Click Start

Take note

Different types of printers have different types of properties. Some of the examples given here may not apply to your machine.

Tip

The Fax is also a "printer". Paper size, grayscales and other "printing" aspects are controlled from here. Other settings are handled from the Mail and Fax Control panel

④ Right click

⑤ Open Properties

All printers have a Paper panel, with Paper Size and Orientation options. Alternative Layouts are normally only found on Postscript printers

On the Fonts panel, if you have the choice, select Print TrueType as graphics – this is usually quicker.

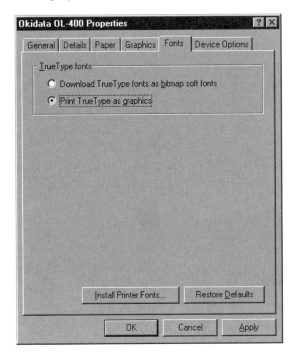

On the Graphics panel, you may have Dithering options. Dithering can give smoother curves and angled lines. Test each option with a page containing a mixture of colored bitmaps and line drawings to see which gives best results on your printer.

Adding a printer

This is a very easy process, thanks to a helpful little Wizard. Windows 95 has drivers for all the major – and many minor – printers in existence at the time of its design. (Drivers are programs that convert the formatting information from your word-processor or other application into the right codes for the printer.) If you have a *very* new machine, you may need to ask the suppliers for a driver for it.

① Open Printers

② Run Add Printer

③ Local or networked?

Click Next at the end of each stage

1 Open the Printers folder.

2 Double click Add Printer.

3 If you are on a network, select *Local* (attached to your PC) or *Networked* printer.

Either

4 Pick the Manufacturer then the Printer from the lists.

or

5 Insert a disk with the printer driver and click Have Disk.

6 Select the Port – normally LPT1.

7 Change the name if you like – networked printers are often given nicknames to identify them.

8 Set this as the default if appropriate.

9 At the final stage opt for the test print then click Finish and wait.

Add Printer Wizard

Click the manufacturer and model of your printer. If your printer came with an installation disk, click Have Disk. If your printer is not listed, consult your printer documentation for a compatible printer.

Manufacturers:
- Epson
- Fujitsu
- Generic
- Hermes
- HP
- IBM/Lexmark
- Kodak

Printers:
- IBM 4029 LaserPrinter PS39
- IBM 4037 5E
- IBM 4039 LaserPrinter
- IBM 4039 LaserPrinter Plus
- IBM 4039 LaserPrinter PS
- IBM 4039 plus PS
- IBM 4070 IJ

Have Disk...

< Back   Next >   Cancel

④ Pick the Manufacturer then the Printer...

⑤ ... or click Have Disk

⑥ Select the Port

Take note

If you have a serial printer, it should be linked to a COM port.

Add Printer Wizard

Click the port you want to use with this printer, and then click Next.

Available ports:
COM1:	Communications Port
COM2:	Communications Port
FAX:	Microsoft Fax Monitor
FILE:	Creates a file on disk
LPT1:	Printer Port
PUB:	Microsoft Fax Monitor

Configure Port...

< Back   Next >   Cancel

Add Printer Wizard

You can type a name for this printer, or you can use the name supplied below. When you have finished, click Next.

Printer name:
IBM 4039 LaserPrinter Plus

Do you want your Windows-based programs to use this printer as the default printer?

○ Yes
● No

< Back   Next >   Cancel

⑦ Edit the name if wanted

⑧ Default?

Managing the queue

When you send a document for printing, Windows 95 will happily handle it in the background. It prepares the file for the printer, stores it in a queue if the printer is already busy or off-line, pushes the pages out one at a time and deletes the temporary files it has created. Nothing visible happens on screen – unless the printer runs out of paper or hits other problems.

This is fine when things run smoothly. However, if you decide you want to cancel the printing of a document, or have sent several and want to push one to the head of the queue, then you do need to see things. No problem!

1 Open the Printers folder.

2 Right click the active printer and select Open from its menu.

❑ To change the order

3 Select the file you want to move.

4 Drag it up or down to its new position.

❑ To cancel printing

5 Select the file(s).

6 Press [Delete] or open the Document menu and select Cancel Printing.

① Open Printers

② Open the active printer's panel

④ Drag up or down

③ Select the file

⑤ Select the file

⑥ Cancel Printing

Basic steps

1 Open the Printers folder.

2 Open the folder containing the document file to be printed.

3 Arrange the windows so that you can see both clearly.

4 Drag the file across and drop it on the printer icon.

Tip

Combine this technique with Quick View, so that you make sure you print the right thing. It makes for a quick and easy way to output existing files.

Direct printing

You do not necessarily have to load a document into an application to print it. Windows 95 can print many types of documents directly from the files. Bitmapped graphics (.BMP files), plain text and the documents from any Microsoft Office application can be printed in this way, as can those from other newer software.

① Open Printers

③ Arrange the windows

② Open the file's folder

④ Drag and drop onto the printer

Take note

You can use this method to print on machines that are not connected to your PC. Simply store the document file on floppy and drag it onto the printer icon on the PC attached to the printer you want to use.

Summary

❑ Printer settings can be adjusted if wanted. The Paper, Graphics and Font options should be checked.

❑ Adding a new printer is easy, thanks to the Wizard. Windows 95 is equipped with drivers for almost all printers currently in use, though you may need a manufacturer's disk with very new models.

❑ Printing is handled in the background, so that – apart from slowing things up a bit – it does not interfere with your other work.

❑ Files are stored in a queue before printing. You can change their order or delete them if necessary.

❑ You can print a document directly, rather than through its application, by dragging the file to the printer icon.

12 Useful tools

The Clipboard

The Clipboard is a mechanism for copying and moving text, graphics, files, folders and other types of data within and between applications. Whatever you are doing in Windows, it is always at hand and always used in the same way.

Any Windows application that handles data in any form has an Edit menu. This always contains three core options – Cut, Copy and Paste – plus varying others. You can see these on the two Edit menus shown below.

● Cut removes a selected block of text or object, and transfers it to the Clipboard's memory.

● Copy takes a copy of the selected item into the Clipboard, but without removing it.

● Paste copies whatever is in the Clipboard into the current cursor position in the application.

Basic steps

❏ To Cut

1 Select the text or object.

2 Open the Edit menu.

3 Click Cut.

❏ To Copy

1 Select the text or object.

2 Open the Edit menu.

3 Click Copy.

❏ To Paste from the Clipboard

1 Place the cursor at the point where you want the selected item to be inserted.

2 Open the Edit menu.

3 Click Paste.

The Edit menus from Paint (left) and WordPad (below). The core options are always there.

Tip

See page 67 for copying files and folders through the Clipboard.

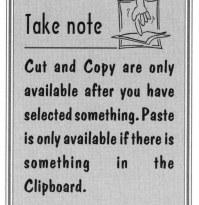

Take note

Cut and Copy are only available after you have selected something. Paste is only available if there is something in the Clipboard.

Basic steps

To select text

1 Place the text cursor at the start of the block.

2 Drag the pointer to spread a highlight over the block.

3 You are ready to Cut or Copy.

To select one object

1 Click on it to get handles around its edges.

To select a set of adjacent objects

1 Imagine a rectangle that will enclose all the objects.

2 Place the pointer at one corner of this rectangle.

3 Drag the broken outline to enclose them all.

4 Release the mouse button and check that all have acquired handles.

Selecting for Cut and Copy

These techniques should work with most Windows applications. Some will also offer additional selection methods of their own, which may be more convenient in some situations.

You normally select text by dragging the pointer over the desired block of characters.

The highlight shows the selected text.

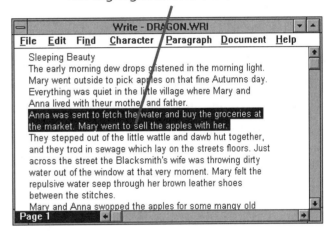

With DTP, or other applications that work with objects – including the cells of spreadsheets and tables – you select a single object by clicking on it, or a group of objects by dragging an outline around them all.

Selected objects are usually indicated by handles.

The enclosing outline

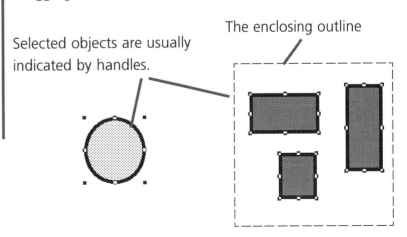

137

Copying the screen

When a PC is in MS-DOS mode, pressing [Print Screen] will send a copy of the screen directly to the printer. When you are working in Windows, the copy goes to the Clipboard. This gives you the chance to edit it before printing, or to pass it on to an application.

● [Print Screen] copies the entire screen.

● [Alt]-[Print Screen] copies the active window.

The screen snapshot can then be pasted directly into a suitable application – a graphics or DTP package, or a word-processor that can handle graphics. If you want to edit it first, paste it into Paint. The screen samples in this book were all produced by capturing the screen or window, and editing as necessary in Paint.

Tip

If you want to see what is in the Clipboard, use the Clipboard Viewer on the Accessories menu. Note that it cannot display the formats used by some applications, though it can hold the data safely.

❑ Copying the screen

1 Tidy up the screen, removing or minimizing unwanted windows, and arranging the others to focus your message clearly.

2 Press [Print Screen].

3 Move to the application into which you want to insert the snapshot, or to Paint.

4 Open the Edit menu and Paste.

❑ Copying a window

1 Adjust the size of the window to fit text or image you want to display.

2 Hold [Alt] and press [Print Screen].

3 Paste the snapshot into the target application.

Basic steps

Character Map

The Character Map

1 Go to the Accessories menu and select Character Map.

2 Select the Font.

3 Click on a character to highlight it.

4 Click [Select] to place it into Characters to Copy.

5 Go back over 3 and 4 as necessary.

6 Click [Copy] to copy to the Clipboard.

7 Return to your application and Paste the characters into it.

This shows the full set of characters that are present in any given font, and allows you to select one or more individual characters for copying into other applications. Its main use is probably for picking up Wingdings for decoration, or the odd foreign letter or mathematical symbols in otherwise straight text.

The characters are rather small, but you can get a better look at a character by holding the mouse button down while you point at it. This produces an enlarged image.

② Select the Font

③ Highlight a character

⑥ Click Copy

④ Click Select

Hold down the button to magnify

Note the keystroke

Tip

If you are going to use a character often, learn its keystroke. This is shown at the bottom right. For Alt+ ones, hold [Alt] and type the number on the Number Pad.

The Phone Dialer

I find this very useful. It gives one-touch dialing – more reliably than the speed dial on my phone, which has the memory of a goldfish. Phone dial does not forget, and entering and editing numbers is easy.

To find Phone Dialer, click ▣Start point to Programs then Accessories.

❏ **Entering a number**

1 Click on a blank button.

2 Enter the name and number in the Speed Dial panel.

3 Click [Save]

❏ **Editing a number**

4 Open the Edit menu and select Speed Dial.

5 Click on the contact to change.

6 Edit as required.

7 Click [Save]

Pick a blank

Click Save

Enter the name and number

Use Edit – Speed Dial

Pick the contact

Edit

Click Save

140

Basic steps

❑ Dialing

Either

1 Select a contact.

or

1 Enter a number directly on the keypad.

2 Pick up the phone.

3 Click [Dial]

4 Wait for it to dial the number and give a high pitched tone, then click [Talk]

③ Click Dial

① Pick a contact or dial directly

④ Click Talk

Isabel Schoenemann
5 Post Ave Apt 21
New York NY 10034-5841

MS-DOS programs

Some DOS programs can be run directly from within Windows 95, simply by adding them to the Start menu. Set them to run in a Window, rather than Full Screen, to give you access to the Edit facilities. The number of screen lines and the font can be adjusted to suit yourself.

Basic steps

- ❑ Setting up
- **1** Open the Properties dialog box for the program's shortcut.
- **2** Switch to the Screen panel.
- **3** Check that the Usage is set to Window.
- **4** Set the Initial size.

② Open the Screen panel

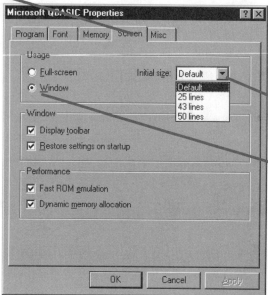

④ Set the Size

③ Run in a window

Turn on the Toolbar in DOS windows for easy editing and font control.

The MS-DOS Prompt

This gives you the standard DOS C:> prompt. Use it for those programs that will not run from a shortcut, or that are rarely used.

Make sure the MS-DOS Prompt is set to run in a window.

Copy and Paste in MS-DOS

❑ Copying

1 Open the Control menu.

2 Select Edit, then Mark.

3 Highlight the text you want to copy.

4 Open the Control menu again and select Edit – Copy.

5 Switch to your target application and paste the text there.

There is an Edit item in the Control menu in DOS windows, and a set of Toolbar icons that can be used to copy text between DOS and Windows applications. Pasting is the same as normal, but to copy you must first use Edit – Mark to highlight the block of text. To do this, imagine a rectangle that encloses the text. Point to one corner and drag the highlight to the opposite corner.

① Open the Control menu

② Select Edit – Mark

③ Highlight the text

④ Select Edit – Copy

Fonts

The **A** icon on the Toolbar takes you to the Font property panel of the MS-DOS window. Note that the window's size varies with the font size, so that it holds the same quantity of text. The Window Preview shows the size of the window relative to the whole screen.

Take note

Some DOS programs cannot be run in a DOS window or from the Prompt. For these, you will have to shut down and exit to DOS.

Summary

❑ The Clipboard is used for copying text and graphics within and between programs, and for copying files and folders across disks and folders.

❑ Text can be selected by dragging a highlight over it.

❑ Individual images and files can be selected by clicking on them. Groups of objects can be selected by dragging outlines around them.

❑ An image of the screen can be captured by pressing [Print Screen]. An image of the current window can be captured by pressing [Alt]–[Print Screen].

❑ The Character map allows you to select special characters from a selected font, to paste into an application.

❑ If your phone is connected through your modem/PC system, you can use the Phone Dialer for quick and easy dialing.

❑ MS-DOS programs can be run directly from shortcuts, or through the MS-DOS prompt. In either case, they should be set to run in a window, not full screen, to get access to the cut and paste facilities.

Microsoft Plus!

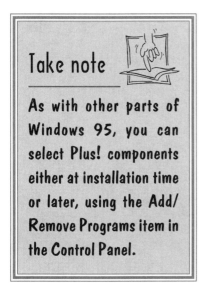

Take note

As with other parts of Windows 95, you can select Plus! components either at installation time or later, using the Add/Remove Programs item in the Control Panel.

Microsoft Plus! is a package of add-ons to Windows 95, aimed mainly at those users with more powerful systems. It is a mixture of utilities and fripperies.

DriveSpace3 is an advanced disk compressor, and useful if you have a hard drive larger than 250Mb. (See page 99.)

System Agent allows you to set up routines to perform housekeeping chores at scheduled times or when the PC is idle. This is probably most useful on networked machines, or those with multiple users.

The Internet Jumpstart Kit will give you what you need to connect to the Internet. Useful if you do not already have a connection.

Desktop themes are covered on the next page.

Dial Up Networking Server is for those that want to let other remote users link into their system.

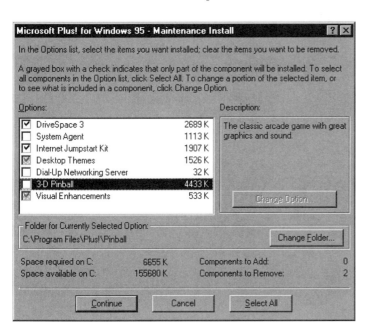

3-D Pinball is a game. Cool graphics and slick action – as long as you like pinball.

The Visual Enhancements include better representation of fonts, animated pointers and a routine to stretch a Wallpaper image to fill the screen. For these, your screen must handle at least 256 colors; some need more than that.

A Desktop theme links wallpaper, icons, pointers, sounds and other parts of the desktop around a common concept. They are cleverly done but purely decorative. Some will work on 256-color screens; others require higher color resolution. *Dangerous Creatures*, right, has hilarious icons and pointers.

Microsoft Plus! adds another panel to the Display Properties to handle the visual enhancements and themed icons.

Note that the Stretch Wallpaper to fill screen option does precisely that – if the graphic that you are using as a wallpaper is not the same proportions as the screen, it will be distorted.

Index